inside
MALTA
AND GOZO

Published by
Miranda Publishers
139/3 Tower Road
Sliema, Malta
e-mail: mirandabooks@onvol.net
www.mirandabooks.com

First published 2005
Reprinted 2008

Photography: **Daniel Cilia**

except pages 56, 57, 86, 87, 108, 109, 110, 111,
158, 159 (Enrico Formica)
and page 145 (Kurt Arrigo)

Design: David Alderton

Production: Promotion Services Ltd, Malta

Scanning: Scancraft Studios, Malta

Printed in China

ISBN 978-99909-85-17-7 (hard-back)
ISBN 978-99909-85-18-4 (paper-back)

inside MALTA
AND GOZO

The Maltese Islands are famed for their history. Man first set foot here around 5,000 BC, arriving from Europe across a land bridge believed to have joined Malta to Sicily at that time. They built the first free-standing stone edifices in the world. Since that momentous time, as the Islands are at the crossroads of the Mediterranean, their strategic position made them coveted by all the major forces in the region, including the Romans, Carthaginians and Aghlabid Arabs until they were given to the Order of St John whose own heroic feats would earn the Knights international renown as the Knights of Malta and after the Great Siege of 1565 enshrine Malta's place in history. The Islands have a wealth of places of interest that span centuries and different cultures, war and peace, religion and art, and, to give them their distinctive image, they have a rocky coastline with a scattering of beaches surrounded by clear blue sea and a countryside landscape that is rich with fertile valleys, terraced fields and villages dominated by parish churches. These are islands to be explored and enjoyed.

Contents

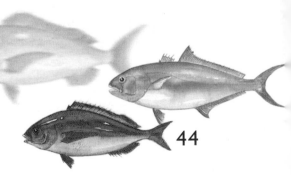

44

Dedicated to
St John

The Knights of the Order of St John referred to their religious headquarters, the Conventual Church of St John, as *"la nostra chiesa maggiore della Sacra Religione Gerosolmitana"*. It was the main beneficiary of their many endowments and was enriched with only the finest works of art.

Gerolamo Cassar, the noted Maltese

simple, with a central nave and two side aisles. The huge vault over the nave is articulated into six bays, a division that reflects the sectioning of the aisle into six side-chapels, which are separated by heavy buttressing to relieve the downward thrust of the vault. This system of powerful structural support is seen as being indicative of Cassar's uncertainty at the daringly innovative scale of the church he had designed.

In 1598, 20 years after the main structure was completed, the sacristy rooms were built to the left of the main entrance, on a rectangular plan with a coffered vault. Today, the main sacristy houses a gallery of Mannerist paintings that originally hung as altarpieces in the side-chapels. Mattia Perez d'Aleccio's *The Baptism of Christ* was the main altarpiece until 1701, when it was replaced by the group of marble sculptures. Other remarkable paintings are Stefano Pieri's *The Flagellation of Christ*,

Prior to 1607, news of Caravaggio's fame in Italy had reached Grand Master Alof de Wignacourt, who offered sanctuary to the temperamental artist while he was awaiting a papal pardon for a grave misdemeanour. Caravaggio was to spend just over one year in Malta, where he completed several paintings.

ITS FAÇADE APPEARS EXTRAORDINARILY SIMPLE, PERHAPS EVEN FORBIDDING — ALMOST AN EXTENSION TO THE HIGH-WALLED BASTIONS THAT FORTIFY VALLETTA.

architect who designed the building, gave the interior an austere appearance, affording only shallow flutings to pilasters and a coffered vault. This sobriety was partly relieved by renaissance floral wall decorations, some of which can still be seen on the wooden panels which surround the main altar.

The plan of the Church is similarly

and Antoine de Favray's portrait of Grand Master Pinto.

The Oratory – which was intended for the knights' private devotions, and for the instruction of novices – was completed in 1605. This simple rectangular structure is the setting for a breath-taking painting, *The Beheading of St John*, by Michelangelo Merisi da Caravaggio (1573–1610).

THE TRAINED EYE WILL RECOGNISE L.B. ALBERTI'S 'GOLDEN RULE' OF HARMONIOUS PROPORTIONS, ARTICULATED BY SPARTAN PILASTERS AND FLANKED BY THREE-STOREY TOWERS ELEGANTLY CAPPED BY MULTI-FACED SPIRES.

THE STUNNING CATHEDRAL INTERIOR   opposite page: **MATTEO PEREZ D'ALECCIO'S 'THE BAPTISM OF CHRIST'**

Less than a century after its completion, the Conventual Church was transformed into a jewel of high Baroque art at the hand of Mattia Preti (1613–1699). Preti was a renowned southern Italian Baroque artist from Calabria, who was drawn to Malta by a commission to paint a portrait of the Grand Master. In 1659, he came to an agreement with the Venerable Council of the Order, for the redecoration of the interior of St John's. This agreement was to establish his unrivalled status as the leading artist in Malta to the church. Preti proposed a number of structural alterations, including the widening of the oval windows on either side of each bay in the vault to let in more light. A small passageway was cut into the wall separating each chapel and this resulted in a dazzling vista of doorways, as one looks down each side-aisle.

Preti was also to convert the Oratory from its original stark, meditative arrangement to a grandiose statement, with Venetian-style gilt ornamentation and a beautiful marble altar. The heavily gilded carvings of the vault and arch were the setting for three virtuoso paintings which he undertook. They are feats of illusionism, depicting scenes from the Passion of Christ. Later additions to the Oratory included the sumptuous marble covering of the piers and the monumental portal. The fine bronze *tondo* by Ciro Ferri (1634–1689) that is affixed to the altar, and the extraordinarily accomplished marble head of *St John the Baptist*, are but two examples of the munificence of individual knights who made significant contributions to the embellishment of their conventual church.

In 1661, Preti began his major artistic project: the vault paintings that depicted the cycle of the life and martyrdom of St John the Baptist, patron saint of the Order of St John. This fabulous work is a tour-de-force of Baroque decorative art and has been described as the culmination of Preti's artistic experience that drew on his studies of Roman and Venetian art. He ingeniously utilised the arrangement of the six-bay vault by sub-dividing each bay into three

sections. This afforded 18 vignettes, each one showing an episode from the saint's life. The vault-paintings also include representations of personages, saints and martyrs of the Order, painted in pairs at the sides of each oval window. Preti painted in oils *a secco* – directly on the stone with almost no preparation of the surface. This awesome cycle took five years to complete and he concurrently orchestrated the redecoration of the entire church. He prepared drawings for the walls of the individual chapels, which were then decorated with highly elaborate

1] VYING FOR PLACE AS PRETI'S FINEST PAINTING IS THIS PORTRAYAL OF LEGENDRY ST GEORGE IN THE CHAPEL OF THE LANGUE OF ARAGON.
2] THE FINE ICON OF OUR LADY OF CARAFA IN THE CHAPEL OF THE BLESSED SACRAMENT.
3] CARAVAGGIO'S RECOGNISED MASTERPIECE 'THE BEHEADING OF ST JOHN THE BAPTIST' WHICH HANGS IN THE ORATORY.
4] DETAIL OF THE LARGE WHITE IVORY FIGURE OF CHRIST CRUCIFIED. IT IS A MOVING PIECE AND IS SEASONALLY PLACED ON THE HIGH ALTAR.
opposite page: THE LIGHT ENTERING THE CHURCH FROM THE BALCONY WINDOW CREATES AN ETHEREAL EFFECT. MATTIA PRETI'S CEILING DOMINATES THE AISLE.

9

THE CONVENTUAL CHURCH OF THE ORDER OF THE KNIGHTS OF ST JOHN IS UNDOUBTEDLY THE MOST MAGNIFICENT ARTISTIC ENTITY IN THE MALTESE ISLANDS AND IT ENCAPSULATES AN EXCEEDINGLY GLORIOUS PASSAGE IN THE HISTORY OF THE COUNTRY.

carved reliefs which give St John's its air of opulence. The side chapels were assigned to each of the eight Langues of the Order and they bear testimony to the lavish attention bestowed by their national patrons. These chapels are individual treasures in their own right, housing some of the finest Mannerist and Baroque funerary monuments, commissioned from the best Roman *botteghe* of the 17th and 18th centuries. Altar-pieces are framed by magnificent architectural arrangements which are the work of noted artists, among them Romano Carapecchia (1668–1738). The magnificent flooring is made up of a collection of polychrome marble tomb-stones, the most ancient dating to the first years of the 17th century, reflecting a 200 year tradition in marble intarsia. The first burials were made in a crypt below the main altar, which contains the remains of the Grand Masters who ruled between 1522 and 1623, earning it the name of 'Grand Masters' Crypt'. The sarcophagi containing the remains of Grand Masters de L'Isle Adam (1522–1534) and de la Valette (1557–1568) were brought here from their original location at the Valletta Church of Our Lady of Victories. The sculpture and carvings are a fine example of the late Gothic sensibilities that underwrote the early monuments of the Order. Another burial place for members of the Order was excavated beneath the Oratory. This Crypt of Bartolott

was named after the Master of the Novices, Don Giovanni Bartolott. The treasures that were once housed in the church, for use during religious ceremonies, are in the adjacent Cathedral Museum.

In the museum the Flemish tapestries are the main exhibit – 14 woven panels that were a gift from Grand Master Perellos (1697–1720) and commissioned from the Brussels atelier of Jodicus de Vos. The set is based on cartoons by Rubens, with one panel designed by Poussin. The tapestries were traditionally hung all round the nave of St John's in June, which is the month honouring St John. Other treasures include a Gothic Reliquary of St Peter with its unique set of 13th century *champlevé* enamel plaques, choral books with illuminated miniatures inscribed on parchment, and a collection of sacred vestments.

from top left clockwise: **A VESTMENT, PART OF A MAGNIFICENT COLLECTION PRESENTED TO THE CONVENTUAL CHURCH BY SEVERAL GRAND MASTERS; A PAGE FROM CHORAL BOOK VOLUME 6, FOLIO I RECTO OF THE ANTIPHONARIES DONATED BY GRAND MASTER HAGUES DE LOUBENX VERDALLE (1582–1595); FLEMISH TAPESTRY: 'THE CHURCH TRIUMPHANT'.**

Valletta

the Islands' capital

Architecturally superb, Valletta was built by the Order of St John after the Great Siege. Foundations were laid in 1566 and the plan was to build an impregnable fortress containing a civilized, elegant city. In fact, one of the most significant aspects of Valletta is that it was architecturally planned from scratch on the virgin land of the Sceberras peninsula that lies between Marsamxett and the Grand Harbour. It was the most strategic position on the island, the one most coveted by the Turks during the siege. Grand Master La Valette made it his for all time. For this reason, Valletta is literally overflowing with palaces, churches, monuments and works of art. Today it may be the commercial hub of the island, but it has retained all of its historical, architectural charm.

Museums and Monuments

THE BASTIONS

The massive bastions wrap themselves protectively around the city and are cited as being among the most fascinating fortifications in Europe. The bastions were completed within five years, an impressively short length of time considering the extensive perimeter, using huge stones and primitive tools. Often there were more than 8000 workers a day. Within the thick walls are tunnels, secret passages and storage vaults. There are further fortifications in Floriana, on the way to Marsa and at Pieta. The best sight of the fortified city is from the sea – there are frequent harbour cruises where boats trace the rocky coastline and the bastions rise powerfully high from the sea. By night, these are floodlit to perfection, a stirring monument to the past, a spectacle of beauty for the present.

ST JOHN'S CO-CATHEDRAL AND MUSEUM

This is Malta's most prized monument to the glorious epoch of the Knights. It was originally the Conventual Church of the Order, the focus of religious ritual and obedient service dedicated to St John, who was patron saint of the Order. In St John's Square, the surrounding space allows a full view of its somewhat austere façade giving the impression of strength and solidity, of

a forthright and noble purpose. For more than 70 years after its completion, St John's remained a vast stone structure, barren of decoration. In 1661, Grand Master Rafael Cottoner commissioned

Mattia Preti, one of the outstanding artists of the Italian Seicento, to decorate the ceiling and redesign the interior.

Once within the portals there is the overwhelming surprise of high Baroque, a startling contrast to the somber exterior. It's a blaze of colour, a cornucopia of decoration: every inch of the stone walls, arches and columns are carved into an embroidered medley of flowers, scrolls, shells, angels, symbols and heraldic emblems, gilded and coloured. The floor is paved with marble slabs, each the tomb of a Knight bearing his coat of arms in intricate inlay. The crypt beneath the Cathedral contains the tombs of de L'Isle Adam, the Grand Master who brought the Knights to Malta, and de la Valette who led them through the Great Siege.

Despite richness everywhere, the eye is directed to the high altar, where Preti's frescoed vault depicts history of the Knights. In the Oratory is Caravaggio's masterpiece *The beheading of St John* which one renowned critic has described as the painting of the 17th century; there is also his *St Jerome*. Both were painted during a 15 month stay in Malta.

The adjacent museum relates solely to the history of St John's when it was the conventual church of the Order. It contains silver, sacred church vestments and beautifully scripted and illustrated choral books. Most of the treasury's priceless riches were plundered by Napoleon's troops in 1798. Fortunately the unique collection of Flemish tapestries was spared. There are 14 pieces, all in mint condition; they were the gift of Grand Master Ramon Perellos at the beginning of the 18th century.

PALACE OF THE GRAND MASTERS

This magnificent palace was the administrative headquarters of the Order of St John, the seat of council, the control centre for matters of state, for military, economic and religious decisions, as well as the formal court of the Grand Master.

Designed by the prolific Gerolamo Cassar, it was completed in 1574 and over the centuries has remained the focal point of government. Plaques and paintings, decoration and furnishings reflect the varied history of the Order,

British colonial rule and the Republic of Malta. Today it is the office of the President and home of Parliament, where a functional space has been converted into the House of Representatives.

The exterior is severe and forceful. The only embellishments – the two Doric portals and the wooden balconies – were added towards the end of the eighteenth century.

The entrance leads almost immediately into a charming courtyard (one of two) with subtropical trees, flowers and a fabled bronze statue of Neptune. Local limestone forms high vaulting, saucer domes and wide corridors. All state rooms are on the first floor; originally the ground floor was reserved for stables, coaches, kitchens, servants quarters and store rooms.

Within the palace is a wealth of splendour. On view are the Corridor, Throne Room, Hall of St Michael and St George, the Red Room and the Council Chamber, which is hung with superb Gobelin tapestries incredibly well preserved. These are world renowned treasures, known as *Les Tentures des Indes* (Indian hangings). They depict in vivid colours jungle scenes recalling the hunting expeditions of a German Prince in Brazil, the Caribbean Islands, India and tropical Africa in the middle of the seventeenth century. At the rear of the Palace is the Armoury. It is unique. There are over 5700 pieces from all over Europe, giving a concentrated view of the developments in weapons up to the 18th century; rapiers, swords, daggers, halberds, pikes and lances, pistols, mortars and small ordnance. Pride of place, however, goes to the armour – which, above all, captures the spirit of the Knights, bringing their world to life. Outstanding is Grand Master Alof de Wignacourt's gold embossed suit weighing 50 kilograms.

THE AUBERGES

These were the living and recreational quarters of the Knights, who were divided into eight langues according to nationality; Auvergne, Provence, France, Aragon, Castille, England,

Germany and Italy. Seven were designed by Gerolamo Cassar between 1571 and 1590. Only five of the original Auberges are still standing and all of these house state institutions.

The Auberge d'Allemagne was demolished to make space for the Anglican Cathedral of St Paul (Independence Square).

The Auberge d'Auvergne was bombed in the second world war, and replaced by the new law court buildings (Republic Street).

The Auberge de France was also badly damaged and was reconstructed as the Workers Memorial Building (South Street).

**Auberge de Castile,
Leon et Portugal**

This is the most beautiful and impressive of the original hostelries. It was initially built in renaissance style,

but was given a new Baroque façade in the mid-eighteenth century when the Knights became conscious of style, status and prestige. It was redesigned by Andrea Belli, a Maltese architect

from Zejtun. The exterior is elegantly decorated with carved stone; a pair of cannons guard the high doorway at the head of a gracious flight of steps. It is ideally situated on the ramparts of the city. For many years it was the headquarters of the British army. Now the office of the Prime Minister.

Auberge d'Italie

Erected in 1574 it has gone through various degrees of alteration over the years and is a far cry from the original design. Situated at the top end of Merchants Street, it now houses the Ministry of Tourism.

Auberge de Provence

Built by Cassar in 1577, it was one of three French Auberges. On Republic Street, it is now the Museum of Archaeology.

Auberge d'Aragon

The first to be built, it is still impressive and is now occupied by a government ministry. In Independence Square, it is worth peeping through the door (visitors are not allowed except on official business) if only to catch a glimpse of the stunning rectangular courtyard, converted into a glass-covered conservatory flaunting exotic plants.

Auberge de Baviere

The Anglo-Bavarian langue was not formed until 1783 and what was previously the Palazzo Carniero became the official Auberge.
It is perched on the bastions at the bottom of Old Bakery Street and is now government offices.

THE NATIONAL MUSEUM OF ARCHAEOLOGY

On Republic Street, it is housed in the

Auberge de Provence and creatively presents collections of the remains of prehistoric settlements: pottery, sculpture, statuettes, stone implements and personal artifacts recovered from Malta's megalithic temples and other sites. On permanent display is the Neolithic Venus of Malta and the

famous Sleeping Lady found at The Hypogeum in Paola. There are also pieces from the Phoenician, Roman and Arab periods.

THE NATIONAL LIBRARY

On Piazza Republikka overlooking the open air cafes, this imposing Baroque building is known as the Biblioteca. The last building of importance to be erected by the Order of St John, in 1796. Its archives boast over 300,000 books and 10,000 priceless manuscripts dating from the 12th to the 19th centuries. Among the papers is the signed Bull and accompanying letter in which Henry VIII proclaimed himself Head of the Church of England. When Napoleon conquered Malta, he ordered all to be destroyed. Fortunately his command was not obeyed, and the library remains a prime and unparalled source of reference for academics.

THE NATIONAL MUSEUM OF FINE ARTS

On South Street, this 18th century palace became a museum in the early 1970s. A patrician, elegant building, it was built about 1570. From 1821 to 1961 it was known as Admiralty House and was the official residence of the British Naval Commander in Chief.

The exhibition of paintings, sculptures, furniture and decorative objects d'art were primarily donated by the Knights and embrace the 17th, 18th and 19th centuries. There are works by Tintoretto, Perugino, Preti, Carpaccio, Ribera, Reni, Valentin, Domenico di Michelino, Mathias Stomer, Favray and Vernet. Of special interest is a section devoted to works by Maltese artists.

THE NATIONAL WAR MUSEUM

Within the walls of Fort St Elmo is an exhibition of World War II relics, from Malta's famous Gladiator aircraft, *Faith*, to weapons, uniforms and vehicles. On the esplanade in front of the fort are the St Elmo Granaries, storage pits with stone lids built by the Knights. There is a similar square in Floriana.

THE MANOEL THEATRE

Originally built as a Court Theatre by Grand Master Manoel de Vilhena in 1731, it is reputed to be the second oldest theatre still in use in Europe. It is a gem of 18th century Baroque design with gilded boxes rising in tiers to the ornate ceiling. In 1960 it was completely and meticulously restored to its original glory. The acoustics are internationally recognized as unique. It is now in use for most of the year (not during summer months) and performances include operas, concerts, plays, ballet and recitals. It is situated on Old Theatre Street. There are tours of the theatre, Monday to Friday.

SACRA INFERMERIA

(The Holy Infirmary) Now The Mediterranean Conference Centre. This was the original hospital of the Order of St John, famous throughout Europe as being the most advanced in matters of medicine and hygiene, with nursing of the highest standard. Constructed in 1574 under Grand Master Jean de la Cassiere, it was one of the first buildings in Valletta, an imposing statement of the basic philosophy of the Order: that of caring for the sick. The Knights took turns in the wards as this was part of their vow. There was an extensive library, a pharmacy and Faculties of Anatomy and Surgery. Of particular renown was the Great Ward, believed, at 161 metres, to be one of the longest halls in Europe. Altogether there were six wards and each patient had his own bed, which was most unusual at that time. It cared for everyone (men, that is, not women) from pilgrims to slaves, the poor and the orphans – of every class, foreigners as well as Maltese. Non-Catholics, however, could not remain in the Great Ward for more than three days if they declined to accept religious instruction from the chaplains. Patients were fed from silver plates. With the departure of the Order in 1798, the victorious French declared the hospital for exclusive use of their troops. They also looted most of the gold and silver. It remained a military hospital when the British ousted the French from Malta two years later. From 1800 to 1920 it cared for the British Forces and played a major role in World War I. The hospital suffered extensive damage in the Second World War, areas of it reduced to rubble. In 1978 it was restored to a spectacular degree. The space was converted into an excellent, fully equipped Conference

Centre, while reclaiming its former architectural glory. This superb restoration won the coveted Europa Nostra Award for its tasteful blending of ancient and modern. Situated at the lower end of Merchants Street, its long severe façade overlooks the Grand Harbour. The main conference hall seats 1,400 people; other additional converted halls provide ideal venues for all types and sizes of conferences, operas, plays, musical performances and exhibitions.

CHURCHES

The capital is dotted with small churches of architectural and religious significance containing a wealth of Baroque detailing and paintings of quality. Worthy of a visit are:

St Paul's Shipwreck Church (St Paul's Street) is one of the oldest churches in Valletta, designed by Gerolamo Cassar it was built to commemorate St Paul's shipwreck on the island. There are impressive vault paintings by Attilo Palombi depicting episodes in the life of St Paul. There is also a magnificent wooden statue of the apostle carved by the famous Maltese sculptor, Melchiorre Gafà (1657) and two significant religious relics: an arm bone of St Paul and a piece of the column on which he was beheaded.

The church is rich in gold and silver sacred artefacts, including an 18th century silver throne.

The Church of St Catherine of Italy (top of Merchants Street) was the church of the langue of Italy to which it was originally joined. Designed in the 16th century, again by Cassar, it was dedicated to St Catherine of Siena. In the early 18th century it received a Baroque façade. The interior is octagonal with a fine dome. There is a magnificent painting by Mattia Preti over the main altar.

Chiesa di Gesù (Merchants Street) is one of the most beautiful churches in Valletta. Designed by Francesco Buonamico, its structure and internal

design resemble the Jesuit Church of Rome which also has the same name. The church owns a great number of remarkable paintings and sacred objects. It was the Jesuits who founded the first university of Malta in 1592, the Collegium Melitensia Societatis Jesù, for the teaching of letters, philosophy and theology.

Our Lady of Victories (opposite the Church of St Catherine) was the very first building to be erected in Valletta and is therefore the oldest church in the city.

For many years it was the parish church. In the 17th century it was embellished with the present façade. Above the entrance is a bust of Pope Innocent XI.

The Carmelite Church (Old Theatre Street) dominates the skyline of Valletta with its huge dome, 42 metres high. The original church of the 16th century was badly damaged in the war, and this reconstruction was begun in 1958. The reinforced concrete dome is entirely covered with Malta stone. It houses paintings by Calì, Preti and

de Arena as well as a statue of Our Lady of Mount Carmel.

THE GRAND HARBOUR

The best vantage point is from the Upper Barrakka Gardens near the Auberge de Castille. The panorama is incomparable, encompassing the complete strategic outlay of Grand Harbour. The expansive sweep from left to right takes in the breakwater entrance to the harbour, Fort Ricasoli and Bighi, then Fort St Angelo and The Three Cities of Vittoriosa, Cospicua and Senglea.

Also facing the Harbour but on the bastion closer to its entrance are the Lower Barrakka Gardens. The gardens overlook the commemorative bell unveiled by Queen Elizabeth on the 50th anniversary of the award of the George Cross to Malta in 1992.

~ **Vittoriosa** ~
first home of
the Knights

Vittoriosa, the centre of Maltese culture and of urban life before Valletta was built in the late 16th century, lies in the shadow of Fort St Angelo, the stronghold which defended the Grand Harbour in the days of the Knights of the Order of St John. The crucial role it played during the Great Siege of 1565, when Malta was under attack by the forces of the Ottoman Empire, was formally recognized when the name, which means 'victorious', was bestowed on the town, replacing the original appellation of Borgo, or Birgu. Curiously more than four centuries later, Birgu is still the name used by the Maltese.

Together with Senglea once (L-Isla) and Cospicua (Bormla), Vittoriosa is enclosed by some five kilometres of fortifications in the district known as Cottonera. Collectively they are also referred to as The Three Cities, honorific titles bestowed on them by the French garrison commanders during France's brief rule of the islands. They are structurally indistinguishable, with boundaries that merge and with similar architecture. They enclose Galley Creek, the Knights' shelter, and have

over the centuries sheltered and catered to the needs of other countless multitudes of vessels and of seafarers. The atmosphere is that of a typical old southern Mediterranean port town, with vivacious and vociferous people and much hustle and bustle in the narrow streets, particularly on market day.

Vittoriosa is a medieval city, but its growth was not haphazard. It was preplanned, and all its thoroughfares lead to the main square. It was conceived along splendid lines and housed the various auberges and administrative buildings of the Knights of the Order of St John before these moved to La Valette's new city, Valletta. For over 40 years, the winding streets and alleys of Borgo were thronged by Knights coming from many different countries, their retainers, and crowds of merchants, money-lenders, sailors and tradesmen. At that time, it was considered the administrative hub of the islands, a busy centre through which flowed the traffic of trade, commerce, shipping, and war.

Many of the buildings of those times,

including the Knights' Hospital, the Armoury, the Treasury, and some auberges and palatial residences, still stand despite the heavy destruction caused during the Second World War aerial assaults.

The most important building to see is the Palace of the Inquisitor. The Inquisition came to Malta in 1574, (and came to an end in 1798, when Napoleon Bonaparte reached Malta and established French rule). The Inquisitor was the third authority in the country, with the Grand Master and the Bishop.

The Inquisitor's Palace, which was rebuilt in 1660, originally served as a court of civil law, and was known as the Castellania. Continuous internal reconstruction over the centuries has rendered the interior somewhat complicated and maze-like. The cloistered courtyard is a remnant of the Siculo-Norman style of architecture and is the oldest part of the palace. With the end of the Inquisition, the palace fell into a period of disuse until taken over by the British as an Officers' Mess, a role it retained until the 1930s, when it was handed to the museum authorities. The palace was then restored, and furnished appropriately. Another interesting building is the Auberge d'Angleterre. This was purchased in 1534 by an English knight, Sir Clement West, from a woman called Catherine Abela, who was married to a slave of the Order of St John. He donated it to the Langue of England. A separate apartment inside the building housed the Pilier, who was the head of the Langue. An inventory of furniture and of silver items dated 1559, suggests that the auberge was not lavishly appointed. The English knights were not particularly numerous and were generally the younger sons of aristocratic families. After Henry VIII's split with the Roman Catholic Church, and the rise of Protestantism, their numbers declined. By 1601, there was just a single English knight serving in Malta for though the Langue was re-established by Mary Tudor in 1557, it was suppressed the following year by Elizabeth I. When the headquarters of the Order of St John were moved to Valletta, no English auberge was built, for the Langue was never revived.

Other buildings of note are the Bishop's Palace, the Holy Infirmary, the one-time residence of the Greek Papas who catered to the spiritual needs of the Rhodian community at the time of the Knights, the Palace Armoury, the Treasury Palace, the Palace of the Captains-General of the Galleys, the Università Palace, the former residence of the Chaplains of the Order of the Knights of St John, the former residence of the public executioner (the executions took place in the main square), and Bettina Palace, which is now a private residence and which may only be seen from the outside. A narrow street called Governor's Palace Street was once the Jewish ghetto, but after extensive war damage this was replanned and is no longer recognisable as such.

There are also several religious buildings which can be visited. Foremost among these is the church of St Lawrence, which as a parish dates back to 1090. The present building was constructed in 1696 by the well-known Maltese architect Lorenzo Gafà. The works of art which it contains are particularly noteworthy. Other holy buildings are the Oratory of the Holy Crucifix, the Oratory of St Joseph, the church and convent of the Annunciation, the Carmelite Church, the church of the Holy Trinity, and the church of St Philip. The character of Vittoriosa has changed much during the past few decades. During the Second World War, many of the city's residents were evacuated to less dangerous areas. Vittoriosa, because of its proximity to the Grand Harbour and to the vessels of the Allied forces, was a prime target for air raids. The exodus continued even after 1945, and the city developed its present air of decayed splendour. The glory that was is still visible in the beautiful old buildings that once housed the notables of the country continues to hum with life as new residents move in and a splendid marina now caters for large yachts. Its old streets are never silent.

BREAD

BREAD is a universal food, yet every country produces its own, unique, type, Malta is no exception and the village of Qormi has long been renowned as the village of bakeries that provides the bulk of Malta's staple food. According to tradition, the concentration of bakeries in this area is linked to outbreaks of malaria.

The word malaria is derived from the Italian *mal' aria*, literally, bad air, and it was assumed that the disease flourished in foul air. Qormi, lying close to Marsa, with large pools of stagnant water and putrid air, was considered more prone to malaria than other areas. Consequently, it was decreed that bakeries should be built in the area so that the smoke from their chimneys would blow away the disease. Today there is no malaria on these islands, but the bakeries in Qormi still thrive.

A great number of islanders were farmers and produced their own cereal grains. This gave them a large measure of self-sufficiency; after the harvest and threshing they carted their grain to the local windmill and returned with sacks of flour and meal – a small family's annual supply. Some had a quern at home to hand-grind the grain as the need arose. Others had what is locally known as a *mitħna tal-miexi*, a mill for grinding corn rotated by a beast of burden.

As a result, baking remained a domestic skill for many centuries with few changes in either utensils or processing methods. It was only in the late Middle Ages that professional bakers began operating. The government issued regulations on the building of ovens and also passed laws governing the size, the quality and the price of bread. Kneading was done by hand, pressing and turning the dough in large stone basins on one side of the bakery. Until the early 20th century those bakeries that produced large quantities of bread employed young boys to knead the flour by beating it with their feet – which were washed several times before the kneading began.

Naturally this kneading was not considered as hygienic as it might be, and it was eventually prohibited. It was only by the middle of this century that the process was automated resulting in an improved and more varied product. The oven consisted of an enclosed chamber with a wood fire. When the required temperature was reached, the baker would sweep the oven's floor of ashes and then place the dough, piece by piece into the oven. This procedure often resulted in bread having ash stuck to it, which had to be scraped off before eating. Later a separate opening was provided for the firewood on the right of the oven chamber. Thus the oven's base remained clean and the bread ash free.

Nowadays, one walks into a bakery and picks a loaf from the shelves. In olden days it was not that easy. Housewives used to knead their bread at home in a *żingla*, a large earthenware basin, and then take it to the baker. Before taking it, howerver, housewives marked their dough with a piece of pastry in a recognizable motif so that they would get their own loaf back. Every family prepared enough bread for a week. Loaves were big, each weighing around *ratlejn* – 1.6 kilos. If they were smaller they appeared to become staler more quickly.

Eventually bakeries began making their own bread, selling it to anyone willing to pay extra and avoid the toil of kneading at home. Bread was initially sold only from the bakery, but later a

HOBŻ MALTI

weights, ranging from an *uqija* to a *wiżintejn* – 26.5 grams to 7.9 kilograms – were kept in a drawer. A set of knives was affixed to the lid of the box. These were needed when the seller had to cut a piece of bread to adjust the weight. Malta and Gozo had their own typical loaves. The most common thicker bread prepared in Malta was the *tal-maħlut* loaf. This bread was made from a mixture of corn and barley. The flours were sometimes mixed after milling. The best *tal-maħlut* was that produced from corn and barley sown together and also crushed together. This kind of bread was available until the Second World War. It was made from coarse glutinous grain and had an unpleasant colour, but was rich in nourishment and full of flavour. Gozo's bread had a distinctive character; its thick, brown crust was sometimes sprinkled with fine sesame seeds giving it a nutty flavour. Improvements in the commercial production made possible the development of many varieties of bread varying in shape, flavour and preparation. Besides the *tal-maħlut*, several kinds of raised wheat bread made from finely sifted wheat flour

became available. These included *tal-Franciż*, a long, narrow, crusty French loaf; *tal-Ingliż*, a kind of fancy English bread and *tal kexxun*, a pan loaf, like today's pre-packed bread. Notwithstanding the wide availability of bread, there are still people who make their own bread. This is especially true of flat bread, the earliest form which is still common in much of the Middle East and other areas of the Mediterranean. Called *ftira* in Maltese, this disc-like flat and round bread was highly popular in Gozo because it was easily prepared at home on a *kenur*, a stove made of stone heated with twigs. In Gozo the most typical of the island is called the *ftira Għawdxija*, the Gozitan flat bread. It is seasoned with anchovy, tomatoes, oil and then baked. There are several variations such as the *ftira tal-bakkaljaw* with onions, garlic, boiled cod, oil and parsley; *tal-ful*, with beans; *tal-ġobon*, with local cheese; *ta' l-inċova*, with anchovy and *tal-makku*, with white bait rolled in flour, sweet marjoram, sliced onions and spearmint. During Lent, in Victoria, Gozo, many bakeries also sell a *ftira tar-Randan*, a kind of fritter fried in oil with or without anchovy.

member of the baker's family went around the town or village selling bread from a large box on a horse-drawn cart. *Il-karettun tal-ħobż*, as it was called, had a box with several compartments. A measuring scale with two large pans was hung from the upper side and

San Anton

A Grand Master's Palace

The Palace of San Anton was once
the country house of a wealthy knight
of the Order of St John. He created his
villegiatura country retreat to fit his
lifestyle. This was no ordinary knight:
his name was Fra Antoine de Paule, a
man of great fortune who was favoured
with the wealth of the Grand Priorship
of St Gilles. Like his fellow knights of
Provence who ate off silver plates
in their great Auberge, Fra Antoine
'shone' in a worldly sense more
perhaps than in any other.
He was elected Grand Master at the
age of 71 and on the day of his
instalment it is recorded that he
entertained some 600 guests to dinner.
His reign would herald a greater
degree of pomp, ritual and luxury than
had ever been known in the Order
before his name. He had San Anton
Palace built as his private retreat, near
enough to Valletta and city life. The
Grand Master's official summer
residence, the older Verdala Castle,
constructed less than a hundred years

previously by Grand Master de Verdalle,
offered an austere and certainly more
separated atmosphere, whereas his
new villa, created exactly to his own
specifications, with its protected
gardens and fruit trees was a charming
and more desirable alternative.
The Palace's accounts in the archives
of the Order reveal an extensive
retinue including the mandatory maître
d'Hôtel who could dispose of the
luxury of imported Mount Etna ice in
the hottest months of July and August.
Fra Antoine, always flamboyant, used
a carriage preceded by mounted
trumpeters. There were valets and
grooms in his employ and various
domestic staff including a man whose
sole occupation was the baking of
special black bread for the hunting dogs!
Historian Elizabeth Schermerhorn, in
her book *Malta of the Knights*, says that
Antoine de Paul " . . . was of a social,
one might almost say, voluptuous
temperament. He introduced a greater
degree of ceremony to the court than

27

any of his predecessors." She lists the retinue of the new Grand Master as follows:

I Seneschal (Knight in charge of household), I Maître d'Hôtel, I butler, I steward, valets-de-chambres, I keeper of the storeroom, 3 cooks, 5 scullions (kitchen maids), pantry servants, I miller, I man to distribute the corn, I man to compound the corn, 6 bakers, the bakery retinue, I coffee maker, I rat catcher, 4 valets, 12 pages, 4 chaplains, 2 physicians, book keepers, 3 secretaries (to cope with the 3 main languages in the Order), I confessor, 12 grooms, I gamekeeper (in charge of hunting permits), I fencing master, I grammarian (for the pages), I clock regulator, I house carpenter, drummers, trumpeters, I wigmaker, 8 chasseurs (hunters), palace guards, archers, guardians of the Palace slaves.

This was the end of the first quarter of the 17th century, a time which saw change: change resulting from the tensions between the traditional, religious tenets of the Order facing the secular ideals as worldly aspirations gained ground.

The knights never forgot their aristocratic backgrounds; the concept of nobility was flaunted with pride to the end. They suffered attacks on their revenues throughout their history and perhaps most significantly from the confiscations by Henry VIII in Britain, to the freezing of incomes under the French Revolution. They were always vulnerable, but their architecture remained living evidence of the splendour of their times. San Anton was a respite, almost a folly, a place to forget one's worries on a long cool and airy *piano nobile* situated over the servants quarters and stables in positively blissful herbaceous surroundings.

The problems did not go away of course, and by the end of the 18th century they were not confident enough to shut the doors against the Napoleonic troops. Grand Master Hompesch is much maligned for his weakness in face of Napoleon's demands although it was the French Knights in league with Napoleon, who advised him to do so.

A letter has survived among the papers of General Sir George Whitmore which gives a particularly intimate glimpse of the atmosphere at San Anton during the plague of 1813.

By this date, although not yet ratified by the Treaty of Paris, the British were firmly in control of the islands and had no intention of returning them to the knights. George Whitmore was honest and decent: a military man, an artist and an engineer. His responsibilities were manifold including the creation of Bighi Hospital, the restoration of the palaces and almost the total elimination of plague. He collected letters which he hoped to read in his

house in Cheltenham during his retirement – the following is the one that has survived. It was written by the Maître d'Hôtel of San Anton to his equivalent at the Palace in Valletta. The contents speak for themselves.

St Antoni 3 August 1813

Mr Dubruhl,

I have sent you my accounts and the number of animals sent to the Palace and what remains of my stock.

I am laying in for two months Stock as things seem to be getting scarce and there is no Hempseed to be got nor Indian corn, so I have bought 6 salmi of barley (very fine barley indeed) at 20 Sc per salm. Last summer I paid 30 for it and it will soon be 30 again. I have got in 18 salmi of Bran. My stock is all doing very well. The Bullock will soon be well I hope, the old Boar broke the door down in the night and almost bit him through the fore leggs and tore him in several places about the belly in a dangerous manner. Had it happened to have been one of the Cows he would have torn her udder off and killed her. I thought it was the best way to put an end to him before he done any more mischief so I beat his brains out with a hatchet and sold him for 4 pence per pound but he was so hard no one could eat him. My family is all in good health and all the people about St Antoni Casal a Lia, Casal Attard and Casal Ballsand not one sick. Excuse my not sending more paper for I have but very little. Our best respect to Mrs Dubruhl and all your family. If you want any melons they are very cheap. If you please to tell his Excellency to send me a little more money I will be very much obliged to you. I am very sorry I could not get your barley ground as their has been no wind since I got it. If you want anything more from here, I think it would be much safer to kill it here and send it to you with the skin off. The Wallnutts are not quite ripe. In about six days more I will send you a very fine pair of pigeons.

Your Most Obedient Servant

W. S. Scott

Alexander Ball who ruled Malta at the start of the British period, took up residence at San Anton. He embellished the palace with a new colonnade and was popular. He amused himself with the entertaining company of Samuel Taylor Coleridge who in 1804 was invited to stay at the palace.

One of San Anton's most illustrious residents was Alfie, Queen Victoria's second son. He was Commander-in-Chief of the Mediterranean Squadron. He had married Marie, Grand Duchess of Russia and daughter of Tsar Alexander. He had once caused a scandal with his youthful indiscretions in Malta and had had to face the ire of his pained and 'let-down' Mama. For the rest of his life however, he behaved. Although not allowed to accept the throne of Greece, he did become Duke of Saxe-Coburg Gotha. His period at San Anton saw the birth of Princess Victoria Melita who would be known as 'Ducky'. She was born on November 25, 1876. She married twice: first to a

grand duke of Hesse and the Rhine, and then, perhaps more significantly, to Grand Duke Kyril Vladimirovich of Russia who would become Head of the House of Romanov and de jure heir to all the Russias.

The more recent history of San Anton Palace is a continuation of the gentility which the place, ensconced in its beautiful gardens, still engenders. British Governors used it as their main residence, and since the inauguration of the Republic, it has been the residence of the Presidents of Malta. Today, so far away from Antoine de Paule's way of life, it survives as an emblem of excellence to herald this little nation's triumphs and to give confidence to who ever lives in it.

Grains of time

Xagħra's rendezvous for two and a half centuries

THE BUILDING OF WINDMILLS IN MALTA BEGAN AFTER 1530
WITH THE ARRIVAL OF THE ORDER OF ST JOHN.

For the past 250 years the skyline
of Xagħra, one of the oldest villages
of Gozo, Malta's sister island, has been
dominated by *il-Mitħna ta' Kola*, the
Windmill of Kola. It has defied the
march of time, the substitution of wind
power by steam and electricity and
still stands as a monument to the hard
working millers of past times.
Windmills, like watermills, were among
the original prime movers that replaced
animal muscle as a source of power.
They were used for centuries in various
parts of the world, converting the
wind's energy into mechanical energy
for grinding corn and other uses. The
so-called tower mills, like the one in
Xagħra, were first developed in France
in the early 14th century and then
spread rapidly throughout Europe.
The establishment of these mills must
have also reached Malta, then an
Aragonese possession, yet it was only
after 1530, with the arrival of the Order
of St John who brought the expertise
for their building from their former

possession of Rhodes, that their number increased considerably. Initially they consisted of a plain massive cylindrical tower rising directly from the ground; later domestic quarters for the miller were added. The Order exercised a monopoly on their building and only millers with a special licence could operate them.

Their number increased considerably when Grand Master Nicholas Cottoner (1663–1680), the sovereign of Malta,

decided to provide every major inhabited area with a windmill for the benefit of the population. He brought skilled artisans from the island of Majorca to advise on the improvement of their structure and mechanism, eventually adopted in all structures. Later Grand Master Manoel de Vilhena (1722–1736) established the *Fondazione Manoel,* a special fund for the building of windmills. One of the first to be raised through this foundation was *ta' Kola* windmill in 1725, named after the original miller. Nine others were raised during de Vilhena's rule. The Xagħra windmill, designed on the same plan of contemporary mills, consists of a quadrangular building

circular slabs, the millstones or grinding stones. These stones, with a diameter of almost two metres and a thickness of about 20 centimetres, made of granite, are placed one above the other. The lower remained stationary while the upper revolved over it. The grain was fed through an aperture in the centre of the revolving stone and was broken and ground into flour as it moved slowly between the two slabs, towards the periphery where it fell into a wooden trough from which it was collected into sacks.

With a system of levers, the upper stone could be raised or lowered thus producing coarser or finer flour as required. This upper stone revolved inside a wooden circular trough that prevented flour from spilling.

A strong upright iron bar passed through the circular hole in the centre of the upper stone, and fitted on its under surface so as to turn it when it motion. The upper end of this bar, which revolved inside a pivot-bearing attached to a horizontal beam, stretched between the opposite sides of the tower, is in turn fixed to a wooden spur wheel geared by a large cog-wheel also made of wood. The spur-wheel revolves at right angle to the cog-wheel,

erected around and incorporating a circular tower about 15 metres high and three metres in diameter. The premises are entered through a main door that leads to a hall, on right there is a room for the reception of grain – now converted into a workshop. Opposite, there is another room for storing flour or grain – now a showplace of windmill mechanisms.

A door opposite the entrance leads to the tower; around the inner walls rises a circular flight of steps leading to the top of the tower. The room behind the tower and those on the first floor accommodated the miller and his family. The mill proper is lodged in the upper part of the round tower. A short distance from the top there is a wooden loft where the sacks filled with grain were raised for grinding by a pulley and where sacks of flour were placed before being lowered.

Ten steps above are the millstone and the gears. Grain was turned into flour by being ground between two large

and this cog-wheel was rotated by the shaft of the sails.

The sails that rotated the millstone are fixed on the top of the tower at right angles to it. The shaft or sail-supporting tail pole is inclined between 5° to 15° to the horizontal. This helps the distribution of the huge weight of the sail and also provides greater clearance between the latter and the support structure. There are six fabric covered, wood-framed wings. Each wing is about 8.5 metres long and consists of a pole with a grid upon it and a sail made of local spun cotton slung on the grid.

As the source of power is the wind, the sails had to be turned squarely into it. This is possible as the horizontal shaft

The slightest breeze is enough to put the mill in motion. The sails impart a powerful turn to the shaft, which rotates the cog-wheel gear with the spur-wheel, which turns the grinding stone. The crushed grain is passed through sieves several times with different meshes to ensure a finer flour. The miller used to inform his customers of a fresh wind by going up on the roof and calling them through the *bronja*, a large cowry used as a sort of horn. Its blowing was a signal to customers that they could bring their sacks of grain to be milled.

The reception room for grain at *ta' Kola* was the village rendezvous. It was here that the villagers of Xagħra met to gossip, to discuss matters of religious or political interest and to while away their time.

The last miller was Guzepp Grech, who died at the age of 87 in 1987. *Il-Mithna ta' Kola* is the best kept windmill on these islands, though it is not in operation today.

to which the sails are attached is supported by a thick wooden circle resting on an iron ring topping the tower. The entire wooden cap of the tower can be made to rotate by winches engaged with geared racks and operated from inside or from the roof by a chain passing over a wheel. It is a very cumbersome operation. When the wind blew strongly the miller had to feather or reduce the sail area so that they would not be ripped apart.

Cryptic tale

There are some wonderful frescoes in
St Agatha's Crypt in Rabat.

Although the Middle Ages in Malta
are shrouded in mystery, two events
of the era have had profound
consequences on the islands. The Arab
invasion in AD 870 was the first and
Count Roger's invasion in 1090 the
second. Roger the Norman
reintroduced Christianity (which was
initially introduced by St Paul in AD 60
but faded in importance due to two
centuries of Arab rule).

Basilian missionary monks, of the
Greek rite, were brought to the island
from Sicily, yet little is known of their
activities during their stay.

However, wherever these monks came
from, they had churches built into rock
faces and several such places of
worship are found around the Rabat
area. In these early mediaeval churches
one can see some of the earliest
examples of wall paintings in Malta.
St Agatha's rock-cut church – or as it
is better known, St Agatha's Crypt – is
one of these.

Tradition has it that St Agatha, fled
to Malta to escape the persecution of
Christians in Catania and the marriage
proposal of Governor Quintianus.
During her three months stay here she
taught Christianity to young children
at the site that later bore her name.
According to tradition, Agatha had
promised her mother to marry

Quintianus after weaving a veil; during her stay in Malta, like Penelope, she used to undo by night the work done by day. When she finally returned to Sicily refusing to marry her suitor, she was tortured and put to death. Because of this the site has always seen great devotion. However, none of Agatha's biographers or the Acts of her Martyrdom relate this story. Consequently, devotion to the site could have preceded the legend. It is known that the Basilian monks from Sicily brought with them the Saints popular on that island, like St Agatha, St Lucy, St Cataldus and several others. Their dedication to such Saints and the sites where they prayed to them could have led to the traditions popularly presumed by the Maltese.

St Agatha's Crypt is situated in the heart of palaeochristian hypogea or catacombs. The church itself was originally a catacomb, much like other burial chambers in the vicinity, and was 'remodelled' more than once. The original staircase led down to a spacious room with a funerary triclinium (a circular stone table with a sloping reclining area used during a funerary banquet) to the left, a corridor ahead is flanked by graves. To the left of the table there is still evidence of a grave with two inscriptions on its sides, both in Greek. The right inscription recalls the name Aurelias. Behind the table, a corridor – whose opening is now blocked by an inscription on stone – ran through the present vestry reaching the tomb that is now the upper portion of the side altar dedicated to Mary, *Mater Divinae Gracie* (fitted and painted between 1881 and 1899). The corridor just opposite the staircase had a beautiful, wide arch before its opening. To the right of this arch was a window grave. The grave opposite the table had pictorial decorations around its façade and a bilingual (Latin and Greek) inscription at the top right corner.

To the right there is evidence of another grave.

It would seem our ancestors did not start excavating the crypt in the ground but enlarged an already existing structure what would have been half its present length.

The painting of the two old fresco panels, which reveal a blend of Romanesque and Byzantine elements, was executed sometime in the 12th century. These paintings represent Mary suckling the child (half of this painting is now missing), St Agatha and a monk. Besides the heads of these figures one sees traces of Gothic lettering and, in one corner, St Agatha, a tiny figure in a praying position.

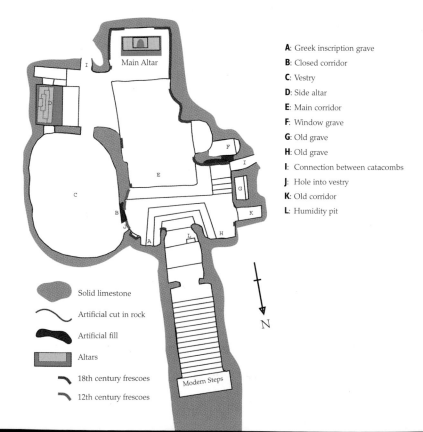

A: Greek inscription grave
B: Closed corridor
C: Vestry
D: Side altar
E: Main corridor
F: Window grave
G: Old grave
H: Old grave
I: Connection between catacombs
J: Hole into vestry
K: Old corridor
L: Humidity pit

Solid limestone
Artificial cut in rock
Artificial fill
Altars
18th century frescoes
12th century frescoes

CUT-AWAY OF HOW THE CATACOMB WAS CONVERTED INTO A CR

In January 1575, a Monsignor Duzzina visited the crypt during a pastoral visit and noted the "many altars" within. All these altars have ceased to exist or were replaced. And according to an inscription, located between two fresco panels, 1575 was also the year when the night's vigil on the saint's feast day was abolished. This may have caused the decline in importance of the crypt until the mid-17th century when devotion of the site was rekindled. In the wake of this new devotion to St Agatha, Monsignor Lucas Buenos,

At some time during the following two centuries the crypt was enlarged to its present length with a vestry adjacent to a part of the present side extension.

Around 1485 another cycle of frescoes was added in Gothic style. The walls were covered with 28 (or more) images of saints depicted either singly, in pairs or in groups of three. These were probably not painted at the same time and art historians tend to identify different artists or workshops responsible for their execution. Some of those portrayed, like St Agatha, St Leonard (holding a chain and symbolic of his love and care of captives) and a bishop saint, are repeated. Others represent saints Margaret, Anthony the Abbot and Blaise. At the edge or in the centre of three panels, is the coat of arms of the Bordino and Falzone families who could have commissioned the paintings.

In 1504, the crypt lost some of its former significance when church was built above it. In 1551, during a siege by an Ottoman force on Mdina enemy troops caused great damage to homes in the area and may have also defaced most of the painted figures in the crypt.

bishop of Malta, donated a statue of St Agatha to the curators of the crypt in 1666 (it is now in the museum). This masterpiece in alabaster was worked in Trapani, Sicily.

In 1670 the church above the crypt was rebuilt.

Between 1721 and 1784 the crypt and the church were neglected and fell into disuse.

An attempt to restore the crypt, costing £17 8s 7d, was made in 1854. Two years later, a new metal gate, costing £56 4s 6d, was placed at the crypt's entrance. In 1870 the Cathedral Chapter decided to revive the complex and restart holding services.

In the nine years that followed (1870–79) the church was heavily restored. The catacombs were cleared from the earth, rubble and debris that had accumulated after they fell into disuse. The link between the catacombs and the crypt was made accessible again and enlarged, and a metal gate was fitted at the entrance to the connecting corridor. The place was usable again for St Agatha's feast day in 1879. After an interruption of a "bit less than 100 years", Mass could be heard again.

The restoration of the frescoes, meanwhile, was carried out "very professionally" in summer 1881 by the local artist Giuseppe Calleja.

In his writings in 1881 Canon P Pullicino makes no reference to the old Romanesque frescoes since, most likely, they were thickly covered with lime scaling and not visible. Caruana, on the other hand, writing 18 years later, noticed the frescoes as some of the lime had fallen off.

The pit between the modern doors of the crypt (which were placed in 1983 to maintain as constant a level of temperature and humidity as possible), was commissioned by Monsignor G Pace Forno probably between 1870 and 1874. More than 100 years later, a charitable group financed the restoration of all the frescoes in the crypt. The work was carried out by George Farrugia of Qormi. He removed all previous restorations, cleaned the frescoes to rid them of the thick salt layers on their surfaces and filled in the missing plaster areas. These were retouched with permanent water colours or just reintegrated in a neutral colour. Finally a coating of synthetic varnish was applied. Thanks to this delicate operation, the many people who daily visit the crypt can admire both the mediaeval structure and its remarkable frescoes.

THE PIGMENTS USED IN THE 19TH CENTURY RESTORATION WERE DIFFERENT FROM THOSE USED IN THE ORIGINAL FRESCOES

The freshest **fish**

The unpolluted waters of the Maltese Islands
are abundant with delicious fish, as well as lobsters, prawns,
crabs, mussels, octopus and squid. Fishing boats go
out daily and the time lapse from sea to plate is often literally only a few hours.

Cerna ~ Grouper

A yellowish brown colour with dark cloudy patches against a pink ground, its maximum length is 100cm. This is a delicious fish, the flesh firm and delicately flavoured, free of bone and suited to many ways of cooking.

Wherever you dine, it is the rare hotel or restaurant that does not offer a wide selection of fish dishes. There are imaginative first courses and sumptuous main ones, both hot and cold. Because of guaranteed freshness, the simplest

cooking methods are used to retain flavour and moisture and to achieve that certain aromatic delicacy so typical of the Mediterranean.

Grilling is preferred, and rightly so, as it is the best way to cook very fresh fish. You will often find *en papillote* suggestions, where the fish, sometimes stuffed, is baked in the oven, wrapped in foil or cooking parchment. For all fish, whatever the preparation, traditional Mediterranean ingredients are used: garlic, olive oil, parsley, occasionally capers and anchovies, often a touch of mint, and always an abundance of lemon.

In general, the Maltese stick to this simplicity, though the more ambitious chefs go for sauces – mainly green and lemon variations, but sometimes they are inspired to create rich shellfish creams.

There are many delicious and spicy dishes with octopus, squid and assorted shellfish, again with liberal use of garlic and herbs. Clams and mussels in a tomato sauce are popular with pasta. There's a really good almost clear local fish soup too called *aljotta*. Seafood salad is always to be recommended, while raw white fish together with octopus and squid in a marinade of oil, garlic and capers is quite special.

Buon appetito!

Lampuka ~ Dolphin Fish

A handsome fish of silver and gold colouring speckled with dark grey dots. Fins are trim and neat. Length can reach 100cm. Lampuka accounts for a third by weight of the whole year's catch in Malta. It is very appetising, full of body and flavour. It responds well to grilling and oven baking. Fillets and steaks can also be fried. Lampuki Pie is a Maltese speciality.

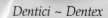

Dentici ~ Dentex

Colour varies according to age but in general it is steel blue and silver with an orangey tint to the pectoral fins. It is speckled with black spots, but curiously these often disappear within a short time of being landed. It is a particularly fine fish, delicious grilled and served with anchovy butter.

Pilot Fish

Although caught in large numbers around Malta, this fish is not very common elsewhere in the Mediterranean. Sleek looking with ribcage markings of grey on a white ground, it has a maximum length of 60cm. Taste is excellent and its firm white flesh can be cooked in many ways. It is often served cold and garnished.

Pagell ~ Red Bream

y longer than 50cm, the back is reddish grey, lly silver. A distinguishing feature is the large spot on the shoulder. Quite a good fish but it n turn dry when grilled. Chefs often put it in a marinade of olive oil.

San Pietro ~ John Dory

An ugly but distinctive fish with extending jaws and a flamboyant spray of greenish fins. Overall colour is a murky brown and it is usually no bigger than 50cm. Peculiar is a dark spot on either side, rather like an extra eye. Despite its looks, it has a superb taste and its firm white flesh separates easily into four fillets free of bone.

Sargu ~ White Bream

Maximum length is 45cm. It is grey with touches of brown and distinctly marked by seven or eight vertical dark stripes along the back, underneath are touches of yellow. A very tasty fish and good for various ways of cooking.

Spnotta ~ Sea Bass

A streamlined silver fish with a darker back, an almost white belly and a ouch of yellow in the fins. An admirable fish with firm flesh free of bone, it can be as long as 100cm. It holds its shape well when cooked, so is often served cold and creatively decorated. When poached – often in white wine – it can come with a variety of sauces.

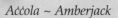

Accola ~ Amberjack

One of the longest fish at a maximum of 125cm, it is fine looking and easily recognisable by the yellow streak running along each side from cheek to tail. Tasty but not easy to cook; however it is to be found grilled, baked and poached.

Past
chimes

Maltese clocks have an interesting history and, even today, the pieces are a legacy of skilled craftsmanship and a Maltese identity like that carved into every Maltese inlaid table, and painted into every Maltese gilded leaf.

Maltese antiques are popular not only because of their decorative appearance, but because they have a value that Louis XV and Chippendale cannot offer: an inherent 'Malteseness' that has particular appeal for local collectors. There is special pride in owning a masterpiece of Maltese craftsmanship that brings with it a wealth of anecdote and an intricate history of previous ownership.

Among the plethora of precious metals, paintings, and furniture that makes hands shoot up at auction sales, is the wall-hung marker of time, known as the *arloġġ tal-lira*. This means, literally, the pound clock – with 'pound' as in money, rather than weight. Fashioned by a gilder, a painter, and a cabinet-maker, these clocks run on metal mechanisms made by the *arluġġar* – a timepiece expert who would also mend pocket-watches and church clocks in his spare time. Fetching thousands of liri on the rare occasions they are offered for sale at auction, these clocks are among the more sought-after antiques. Perhaps this is because their decorative quality is preferred to the sombre portraits of someone else's ancestors.

49

The clocks are distinguished by their decorative appearance: a light-coloured, rectangular face encased in a wooden cabinet with a glass front. The cabinet is generally in a dark colour with Roman numerals marking the hours. The casing itself is decorated with patterns in gold leaf, the handwork of gilders whose techniques and craft are still alive and much-used today. The four corners of the face are ornamented with coloured paintings, usually of flowers, and the space inside the circle of numerals is often enlivened with a landscape or seascape.

On the lower half of the face, an aperture shaped like a smiling mouth reveal the movement of the brass pendulum, and there are often apertures in the sides of the clocks to allow the chimes to be heard louder. Some of the earlier models had just one metal hand – the one that marked the hour. Their owners told the time by listening for the chimes which marked the quarters of each hour. At 12.45 the clock would strike 15 times. The manufacture of each clock was a laborious task shared by at least three craftsmen. Mass production in the various stages of manufacture was not possible because the clocks were usually individually commissioned and produced to fit a particular space on somebody's wall. Each clock was a project in its own right, requiring individual attention and a custom-made mechanism. Curiously, it was the gilder who undertook the commission, not the *arluggar*. A cabinet-maker and clock-maker were then commissioned by the gilder, who took responsibility for the delivery of the finished product, according to his client's specifications. The cabinet was constructed in white deal, a wood fit to take the layers of gypsum which provided a smooth base for the final layer of paint and the gilded decoration. The gypsum was painstakingly applied, a time-consuming task because each layer was allowed to dry before the next one was applied. The mechanism of the clock was a system of weights and wheels, linked by a rope wound

around a pulley. The *mażżri* were leaden; the wheels, brass, and axles of iron. Each piece was handmade by the clock-maker.

The origin of the name *tal-lira* is uncertain and the explanations that have on occasion been put forward are the result of conjecture rather than historical fact. The idea that they were called *tal-lira* because they cost a pound is disputed by the historical researcher and writer Giovanni Bonello who argues that the clocks would have cost far more than that when commissioned. He wrote that the aristocracy and haute bourgeoisie, who probably started the fashion for these elaborate timepieces, would have considered it vulgar to publicise the price of their possessions. The motivation behind the name must be sought elsewhere.

An interesting aspect of Dr Bonello's argument is that the monetary unit then used in Malta was the *scudo*, and not the *lira*. The *scudo* was in circulation in the late 19th century, well after 1825, when the pound was made legal tender. A possible explanation, he speculatesd, may be a type of clock that gained in popularity at around the same time as the *tal-lira*. This clock was known in the USA, in Britain, and in Italy. It was shaped like

a lyre, and in Italy it had the name of *orologio a lira*. The Maltese name is possibly a derivative of this expression, but there is no supporting documentary evidence.

The clocks that once hung on the walls of the homes of nobles and wealthy clerics are rarely on show; many of these antique pieces are in private collections. But some can be seen in museums and public buildings. There are two of these clocks on display at the National Museum of Fine Arts in Valletta, and another two at the Inquisitor's Palace in Vittoriosa. Others are in the Cathedral Museum in Mdina, the National Library in Valletta, and Casa Rocca Piccola, a private residence in the centre of Valletta, that is open to visitors.

Several of the clocks in private collections were put on public display for the first time in 1992, in an exhibition organised by *Fondazzjoni Patrimonju Malti*, the Maltese Heritage Foundation, and held at the Auberge de Provence in Valletta. The exhibition catalogue, with its many photographs, is now itself a collector's item, with a copy deposited at the National Library. The dustjacket carries a reproduction of a painting by Antoine de Favray, titled *A Visit to a Maltese Home*. Surrounded by the many paintings, which hang

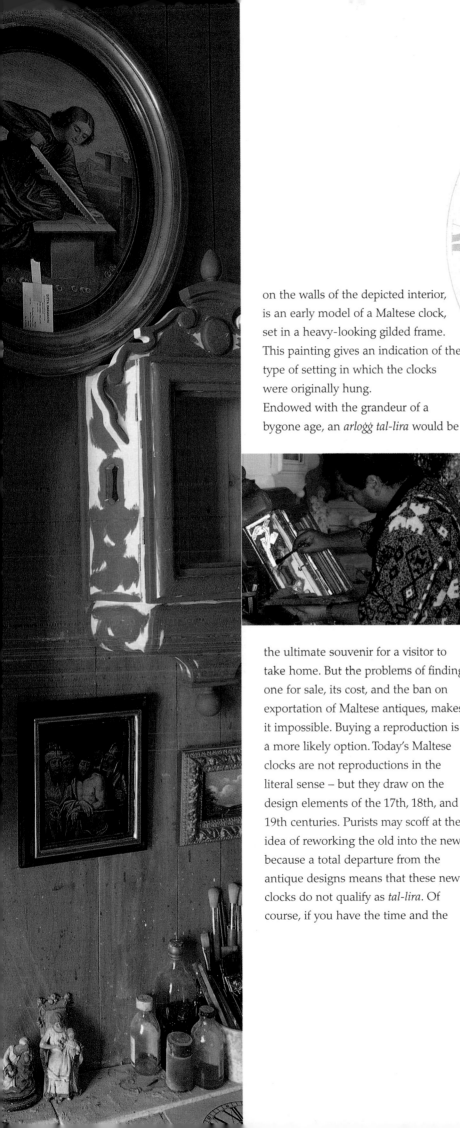

on the walls of the depicted interior, is an early model of a Maltese clock, set in a heavy-looking gilded frame. This painting gives an indication of the type of setting in which the clocks were originally hung.

Endowed with the grandeur of a bygone age, an *arloġġ tal-lira* would be the ultimate souvenir for a visitor to take home. But the problems of finding one for sale, its cost, and the ban on exportation of Maltese antiques, makes it impossible. Buying a reproduction is a more likely option. Today's Maltese clocks are not reproductions in the literal sense – but they draw on the design elements of the 17th, 18th, and 19th centuries. Purists may scoff at the idea of reworking the old into the new, because a total departure from the antique designs means that these new clocks do not qualify as *tal-lira*. Of course, if you have the time and the

inclination, you may consider commissioning an aesthetic and true replica of a favourite old design. The framemaker in the main street of the town of San Ġwann, and the gilder in Valletta's St Christopher Street, are two ports of call for anyone seeking a supplier. Dilettantes who make a hobby of the craft of clock-making might also be persuaded into accepting commissioned work. The best way to locate a supplier is to ask around at antique-dealers and auction houses. Always view samples of the craftsman's work before committing yourself to a commission. Although not nearly as costly as antique clocks, reproductions can cost in excess of Lm100, with the final price dependent on the design and the complexity of the workmanship. One thing you should not expect is chimes. The custom-made cogs, weights, and ropes, with their daily rewinding, have been replaced by mass-produced, quartz mechanisms, powered by pencil batteries. It is perhaps ironic, and a little disappointing, that, of all the craftsmen who were once involved, it is the clock-maker who has been made redundant. But there is comfort in this: owners of these new clocks will be able to sleep at night, without the insomniac's fear of quarterly chimes.

Glory on a hill

No visitor can afford to
miss Malta's old capital city,
originally called Melita or Civitas,
later Notabile or Città Vecchia and
now, simply, Mdina a corruption of its
ancient Arab name, Medina.

For a variety of reasons, the many large groups who daily throng through Mdina's narrow streets are led to just one or two places and the Cathedral. They leave the mediaeval City with a rather blurred image of its spirit and a vague sense of nostalgia for a deeper insight into the city's character.

The long narrow street that divides Mdina in two – its eastern and western halves – is Villegaignon Street, named after the knight Nicholas Durand de Villegaignon. Visitors are generally intrigued by the distinguished personality who in 1551 defended the city against the Turks, but few learn that this central road, in the terrible earthquake of 11 January 1693, witnessed the true weakness and vulnerability of Mdina's structure. Whereas the western half of the city, leading down to Greeks' Gate and

WHAT MOST VISITORS FAIL TO CAPTURE, IS THE TRUE SOUL OF THE CITY, ITS GENUINE SPIRIT AND CULTURE.

the dry moat, built on solid rock, survived the earthquake and still retains its late mediaeval character; the eastern part of the city, built on clay, was badly shaken and was rebuilt during the first half of the 18th century in the new Baroque style of the period. Consequently Mdina is no longer the truly mediaeval town it was before, but partly mediaeval and partly Baroque. One can see this mixture of styles when looking at the beautiful façades on Mdina's main streets, the Palazzo Santa Sofia and Palazzo Falson, Casa Inguanez – the home of Malta's oldest aristocratic family – the Banca Giuratale, Palazzo Testaferrata and Palazzo Gurgion as well as the

Benedictine Nunnery, the Carmelite Priory and the chapels of St Agatha and St Roque.

Mdina's origins are lost in history and prehistory. For thousands of years, however, Mdina was Malta's only urban centre even though Vittoriosa was the island's port.

Mdina's position on a high promontory protected by steep cliffs rendered it ideal for defensive purposes. Its size was originally about eight times its present size and extended into Rabat; in Roman times its limits were surrounded by a ditch, parts of which are still visible behind St Paul's Church in Rabat. The city's size was reduced by the Byzantines

or the Arabs and its entrance consisted of a labyrinth of streets and shops, which was demolished by Grand Master Manoel de Vilhena in an effort to help the city's reconstruction after the earthquake in order to impress the citizens with his princely power.

A few generations ago, Mdina really was a Silent City, its silence being only interrupted at short intervals by the movement of school children who walked from and to Rabat, without the advantages and disadvantages of school transport.

A positive element in today's Mdina is the number of museums and cultural centres it houses. Not a single museum adorned the old city 30 years ago –

many of the works of art currently displayed in the museums were at that time preserved in the city's churches and private houses where they could be appreciated only by a few.

Today the city houses the splendid Cathedral Museum in the building of the Old Seminary across the square from the Cathedral; the National Museum of Natural History in what was formerly the Grand Master's Palace and Palazzo Falson, a new museum housed in this historic palace. Visitors can admire not only the museum exhibits preserved in these historical buildings but also the graceful architecture of the three palaces, eloquently Baroque in the

THE SILENT CITY OF MDINA HAS BECOME THE CITY OF MUSEUMS AND RESEARCH.

case of the Cathedral and the Natural
History Museum and somberly late
mediaeval in the case of the Falson Palace.
Maltese and foreign scholars now also
have the opportunity of delving into a
number of archives, namely those of
the Inquisition together with the
Cathedral and the Episcopal Archives
at the Cathedral Museum, and, at the
Banca Giurale, the national archives of
the Maltese Commune, most of which
cover the days of the Order. These
documentary treasures were closed to
researchers half a century ago.

A number of palaces have been recently
restored at considerable expense, which
partly justifies their conversion into
commercial centres, and, there are
cultural activities in the squares and
streets of Mdina, like the Folk and
Flower Festival and enactments of the
solemn entry of the Grand Master into
the city as well as a number of
concerts in Cathedral Square.

Mdina – the old capital of Malta

This imposing citadel, perched high on a plateau, commands magnificent views over land and to the sea. It is one of the world's finest examples of a medieval walled city still inhabited. It is surrounded by steep vertical bastions and a dry moat. Its history is as old as that of the island and can be traced back more than 4,000 years. Even during the Bronze Age it was a fortified settlement. The Phoenicians built a city wall around Mdina and the surrounding countryside (now part of Rabat) and when it was incorporated into the Republic of Rome in 218 BC it became the island's capital, known as Melita. During the governorship of Publius, a significant event took place in AD 60. The Apostle Paul was shipwrecked on his way to Rome and was taken to Mdina where, it is claimed, he healed Publius' father of a serious illness. Publius later converted to Christianity, becoming the first Bishop of Malta and thus laying the foundations for the island's future and dominant religion. The Saracens took over in AD 870 and separated Mdina from Rabat by a deep dry moat, strengthening the walls and bastions. They renamed it Medina and from that time on the plan of the city has barely changed; its structure and street grid are the same as 1000 years

ago. In 1090 Count Roger, the Norman from Sicily, conquered the island in the name of Christianity and decreed that a new church should be built on the site of a small neglected chapel where Publius' house had once stood. This new Romanesque cathedral was dedicated to St Paul.

When the Knights arrived, it was the refuge of Maltese nobility, unhappy at yet again being passed on to another protector. An agreement was reached to respect the internal autonomy of the city. It came to the rescue of the Knights during the Great Siege and it was the first to rise against the French occupation two and a half centuries later.

For years it has been known as the Silent City because its narrow streets limit traffic. It remains a beautifully tranquil place with perfectly preserved palazzi, historical buildings and monuments.

Museums and Monuments

MAIN GATE

A Baroque triumphal archway with imposing pillars, rich carving and an ornate super structure, originally approached by a drawbridge over a dry moat. It was constructed in 1724 to replace an earlier, simple gate – still visible on the right of the outside wall.

TOWER OF THE OLD STANDARD

In the 16th century, this doubled as a alarm beacon. Bonfires were lit on its roof to warn the population that the Corsairs had been sighted at sea or that the island was being invaded. Now a police station.

THE CATHEDRAL

In Archbishop's Square, the Siculo-Norman Cathedral built by order of Alphonso V of Aragon was destroyed by an earthquake in 1693. The present cathedral rose four years later under the direction of Maltese architect Lorenzo Gafà. It is a splendid work combining a certain Roman Baroque levity with the seriousness expected of a place of worship. The façade is monumental with its Corinthian columns, high central door and towered side wings. Its bold Baroque dome is more like a sculpture, rising high above the hill of Mdina and dominating the countryside for miles. The plan is in the form of a Latin cross with a central vaulted nave and two aisles with small side chapels. The floor is a splendid patchwork of multicoloured marble slabs commemorating leading Maltese ecclesiastics, bishops, prelates, monsignors and canons, as well as prominent noble laymen. Mattia Preti painted the altar-piece of the choir, the apse above and two panels – again of St Paul's life.

THE CATHEDRAL MUSEUM

Many of the treasures not pillaged by the French are on exhibition here. There's a wealth of paintings, sculpture and marble mosaic work, historical vestments, beautifully illuminated choir books dating from the 11th century and a vast coin collection. Paintings and engravings are by Rembrandt, Piranese, Goya, Van Dyck and Dürer, plus an excellent group of Dürer woodcuts. One particular work is a painting of the *Madonna and Child* said to be by St Luke who was stranded in Malta with St Paul in AD 60.

NATIONAL MUSEUM OF NATURAL HISTORY

The impressive Vilhena Palace, with its gracious courtyard and scrolled doorways, houses the collection on two floors. On the first are seashells, birds, insects and butterflies. The ground floor displays geology and the sciences, fossils and fish.

PALAZZO FALSON

On Villegaignon Street, leading to Bastion Square, it is the best preserved medieval building in Mdina, dating back to 1495. Known as the Norman House, it has double arched medieval windows on the first floor and only slits at ground level. It has been restored by Fondazzjoni Patrimonju Malti, the result of an agreement with The Gollcher Foundation which entrusted Patrimonju to restore, re-open and manage the palazzo as a quality museum of fine furniture, silver, paintings, antique carpets and armour.

PALAZZO SANTA SOPHIA

On Villegaignon Street, the basement of this house is assumed to be the oldest in Siculo-Norman style and dates back to 1233. The first floor conversion was added in the 1930s.

CHURCHES

The Carmelite Church (Villegaignon Street) was completed in 1680. It has four side chapels and seven altars. Decorating the main altarpiece is an 18th century painting of the *Annunciation* by Stefano Erardi. The 19th century paintings of *St Simon* and *St Elijah* are by Maltese artist Michele Bellanti. It was here that the riot against the French started in September of 1798, when Napoleon's troops tried to pillage the church's treasures and auction its tapestries to raise money for the Egyptian campaign. The people were furious, hurled Captain Masson, the Commander of the French garrison in Mdina, from a nearby window and initiated the Maltese revolt.

The Nunnery of St Benedict (St Publius Square, just inside the Main Gate) is a somewhat forbidding religious institution. It was founded in 1418 but substantially rebuilt after the earthquake. The site originally was a medieval hospital for women. The sisters have strict rules of seclusion and until recently no nun could leave even after death but had to be buried within its walls. No man is permitted to enter unless he is a doctor and even then only with the permission of the bishop.

Curious stone huts in remote fields to the north of Malta often attract the attention of walkers – but only when they are visitors to the islands. The Maltese take these primitive forms of shelter for granted because they have been there for as long as anyone can remember. But whether they will still be there after another few decades have gone by is doubtful.

The huts, known as *giren* – the singular being *girna* – were built to provide land-tilling peasant farmers with shelter from the midday summer sun and the winter rain, and to provide them with a place for the storage of their tools and dry crops like potatoes and onions. At a time when the fields and the home were separated by some considerable distance and motor transport still in the distant future, this made sense. Those who worked the fields could leave their food and drink in the *girna*, and sometimes even their infant children in a hammock-type cradle strung up between the two walls. With today's amenities, the comforts of the *girna* – such as it was – are no longer essential. Trucks and vans make nothing of distance and can be used to transport tools as well as labourers. They cannot be used for the storage of limited crops, but they can be used to take those crops to a more convenient place. This is unfortunate for the *giren*. They are being neglected because they are no longer needed and no new ones are being built. Because the required building skills are rapidly being lost, when *giren* are repaired, it is in a haphazard manner.

The *girna* is built of rough fieldstones, fitted together dry, and left unplastered. The method of construction is corbelling, a system in which the stones are gradually stepped so as to incline towards the ceiling. The narrow roof opening is then covered with a stone slab. The wall is double thickness, and the space between is filled with rubble and gravel. The roof is covered with fragments of stone, sand, lime, or ground pottery mixtures. One known example was roofed with cane and seaweed, covered with a mixture of hard debris. The interior of these huts is inevitably dome-shaped, but the exterior takes on a variety of forms – circular, oval, square, rectangular. There are 'double' *giren*, and *giren* surrounded by a buttressing wall. Others have a second storey built on top. Some are even incorporated into rubble walls, though these are small and only suitable for sheltering one or two persons. Square or rectangular *giren* serve more practical purposes, particularly for the sheltering or raising of livestock, but circular *giren* are more common because building them is more straightforward. The roofs are flattish, allowing for the drying of tomatoes, figs, and carobs in the sun. Some *giren* have steps leading to the roof.

There are generally no windows, and just one door which faces east to gain maximum advantage of the sunlight. The stones used are those found in the vicinity: loose coralline limestone rocks which lie on the surface and which make field clearance such a labour. *Giren* are built on a rocky outcrop because of the absence of foundations, but the solidity is really dependent on the skilful laying of the stones. The interior is as spartan as the exterior. There may be a few stones as seats, some small openings to allow for the circulation of air, a manger, a recess for a lamp, and a small in-built shelf. *Giren* that were used for the raising of animals had none of these meagre attributes but they did have an enclosure which served as a pen. Most of the larger *giren* were used for this purpose, but they may also have been used for human habitation despite the lack of sanitary facilities or a chimney

old sacks. He refused to change this way of life even when offered a home more in keeping with the times. The last person known to have lived in a *girna*, this time near Dingli, died in 1989. Nowadays they are not used for habitation, because even the most nostalgic of peasant farmers has become accustomed to his creature comforts; but some do contain a bed or a rug, or some primitive cooking

a few in the south. *Giren* are not typical of Malta. A German scholar, Gerard Rohlfs, researched this building method for thirty years and in 1957 published the results under the title of *Primitive Kuppelbauten in Europa*. He noted corbelled stone huts in Italy, Yugoslavia, Sardinia, Spain, Portugal, France, Ireland, and the Hebrides. Only those of Italy and of Malta are flat-roofed. The rest have conical roofs.

for cooking. Cooking was carried out in a separate stone shed, or a portable stove was moved outside, taking its fumes with it.

Salvu Deguara, nicknamed *il-Banker*, lived in one from his early youth until he was persuaded into a home for the elderly – where he died in the 1960s – in a *girna* near Mellieha. He slept on a stack of hay and cooked on a portable stone stove outside his 'front door', which was covered with a curtain of

facilities. This is because they are used for a day or two when work in the fields is particularly intensive.

An 18th century Maltese dictionary gives the meaning of *girna* as 'hovel' giving some indication that they served quite commonly as dwellings.

There are few *giren* in Gozo, which is a strange fact given the similar farming imperatives and topography. There are a number in the fertile regions of the north, west and east of Malta, but only

The Maltese *giren* have been laboriously studied and listed by a Dominican priest, Fr Lawrence Fsadni, who spent many months crossing fields and valleys in his distinctive white robes, reaching many out-of-the-way locations with the aid of the route bus system and volunteers who gave him a ride in cars. The result is a published work, *The Girna – the Maltese Corbelled Stone Hut*, which records the existence of these buildings for posterity.

Someone at the **DOOR**

Ornamental door knockers are by no means peculiar to the Maltese islands, but there is one particular door knocker that is: the stylized brass dolphin. This fleshy-lipped dolphin, which looks more like a mythological fish than the sea-going mammal, once graced many a front door and, today, are often seen displayed in serried ranks in shops designed as a take-home purchase for visitors. Eventually they find their way to the front doors of houses in Britain, Germany and Italy.

Maltese door knockers are usually sold in pairs, because the traditional Maltese front door is double-leafed, not just a single panel. In a custom that has now died out, a household in mourning

would leave one panel closed. Most households now leave one panel closed as a matter of course. It is easier than opening and closing both halves with each trip out of the house.

The door knocker was essential in the days before doorbells. The first doorbells were chain-pull devices which activated a little bell somewhere in the depths of the house, but door knockers, especially the large and heavy variety, were thought to be far more effective. They did not do much good to the door, when they were slammed loudly against it, but doors then were more solid than they are today, and the knockers usually rested on a protective pad of heavy wood, or hit against another piece of brass. Most Maltese door knockers are brass, with very few bronze. They were polished to a brilliant sheen by the housewife or household servants – dirty knockers brought shame as a sign of carelessness. Nowadays, most of the knockers are sold coated with

a protective treatment which makes such polishing unnecessary.

The traditional dolphin, though still an old favourite, has been joined by a more realistic-looking version that looks as though it could leap off the front door. Another traditional design is a simple, solid brass ring, which knocks against a brass stud. Lion's heads are another old favourite – the lion usually carries the knocking-ring in its mouth. There are some reproductions of art nouveau and French Empire styles on sale, which are more elegant and delicate in design.

Relatively new designs include hands in a fist shape, elephants' heads with the trunk used as the knocker, and variations of all the usual themes. There are also reproductions in bronze – treated to look antique – of some of the more elaborate knockers seen on the doors of the noble houses of Mdina.

The very large versions which grace the palatial homes in the old capital

city are proportionate to the enormity of the front doors. A small knocker would have had little effect against these solid doors and the sound would certainly not have carried through the house. Some knockers are so heavy that it takes a strong arm to lift them, and a stronger arm still to bang them effectively against the wood. Yet they are works of art in themselves, and were usually individually cast.

With the coming of the modern door-bell, traditional door knockers have been replaced by simple knob-like handles. Modern, single-panel doors are often made without a space for a door knocker.

The brass knockers live on as a curiosity, having become redundant for communication purposes ("there's somebody at the door!"). But they are a firm favourite with visitors, and, as the numerous signs on shop displays read 'Children are not to touch, please', it proves people cannot resist the good old days.

Pastizzi

Anyone enjoying a hot, mouthwatering *pastizz* is enjoying a recipe that is at least three centuries old. The word *pastizz* is usually translated as 'cheesecake', but this confection is nothing like the traditional sweet cake known as cheesecake, and this sometimes leads to confusion. Malta's traditional flaky and slightly greasy pastry case is savoury and can contain a mixture made of dried peas, known as *piżelli*, as an alternative to traditional *rikotta* cheese.

The *pastizzi's* original diamond-shaped version is still widely available, but this has largely given way to a greater range of shapes and sizes, with bite-sized

> *Anyone enjoying a hot, mouthwatering pastizz is enjoying a recipe that is at least three centuries old.*

pastizzi served even at weddings and formal receptions. What once formed part of the workman's mid-morning break has been adapted to something more fashionable and less messy to eat. Like many of those things which are slotted into a category marked

'traditional Maltese', the origin of the *pastizz* is hazy. The Maltese think of *pastizzi* as being typical to the islands, but there is nothing to prove that they were first made here. Ġuże Cassar Pullicino, the Maltese folklorist, noted in a published article that *rikotta* cheese was known here in the early 18th century. The scholar Agius de Soldanis, in the first known Maltese dictionary, defines *qassata* – another form of *pastizz*, but with a short crust pastry – as "a little pie filled with cheese and eggs". The word *pastizz* may have come from *pastizzu*, which is part of the vernacular tongue used in Sicily and Calabria. Even if *pastizzi* were known here before the first half of the 18th century, it is hardly likely that many people could afford to buy them. The standard of living of the average Maltese was very low, with the majority of families barely subsisting. Homemade versions are equally improbable for few housewives would have taken the time or trouble to make individual cheese pies for an entire family, when making a single large one was more sensible. *Pastizzi* became truly popular at the end of the Second World War, when the general living standards began to climb.

The Maltese usually eat *pastizzi* mid-morning or mid-afternoon, with a glass of tea or coffee (or a cup, depending on the sophistication of the venue). But they are most popular in winter, particularly after Sunday morning mass. In villages where no bars sell them, bakery vans strategically situated by the church parvis on Sunday mornings, attract crowds of customers. The *pastizzi* business has not known better days – the number of *pastizzeriji*, sprouting like mushrooms in the wet season, is a good indicator of the booming trade. *Pastizzi* are inexpensive and delicious to eat, and filling enough to tide a hungry person over to the next square meal.

Machinery has made life a lot easier for those who make them too. The process was more painstaking in years gone by when the cutting, filling and baking took so much time. With no mechanical assistance, cheesecakes would cost more than three times the price they do today. Many bakeries sell a frozen, raw version, which customers put in their freezers at home, then bake when the fancy takes them.

Do current campaigns for healthy eating affect sales? Not much. *Pastizzi* are the classic diet-breaker, though they are worth their weight in calories.

"There is probably no other area of this size in the world with such a number and variety of antiquities" Dr David Trump

During the first half of the present century European archaeologists, puzzling over the similarities between ancient cultures, came up with the diffusion theory; a steady spread westwards of ideas, skills and inventions from the early civilizations of the Near East. In this way the mud-brick ziggurats of ancient Sumeria (the first temples known to man) had influenced the Egyptian pyramids (the oldest stone monuments in the world) and the Maltese Islands megalithic buildings were a mere reflection of the glories of ancient Greece.

There was only one problem. They had no way of confirming exactly when anything had happened. Then came radiocarbondating, an off-shoot of the same research that produced the atomic bomb. The first radiocarbon dates did little to disturb the basic fabric of the theory, but when the technique was refined in the mid-1960s it blew holes through the entire edifice. Small communities, previously considered to be talented imitators, were shown to have been ingenious innovators astonishingly advanced for their time. Malta's temples were the oldest free-standing stone monuments in the world. The Egyptians could no longer be said to have created the oldest free-standing stone monuments because the Stone Age temple builders of Malta had beaten them to it.

THE NEW DATING SHOWED THAT IN THE TINY CLUSTER OF MALTESE ISLANDS, WAY OUT IN THE MIDDLE OF THE MEDITERRANEAN, A PEOPLE WITHOUT A WRITTEN LANGUAGE OR KNOWLEDGE OF ANY KIND OF METAL, HAD RAISED VAST, HIGHLY SOPHISTICATED STRUCTURES SEVERAL HUNDRED YEARS BEFORE THE EGYPTIANS BEGAN WORK ON THEIR OWN TRIUMPHS IN STONE. THEY HAD BEGUN BUILDING AROUND 3600 BC AND CONTINUED FOR OVER A THOUSAND YEARS.

They built their temples singly and in groups, added to them, embellished and enlarged them. Their richly decorated interiors were previously thought to have been inspired by the great Greek civilizations of Crete and Mycenae, but it is now clear that Malta's temple culture had flourished and died before the Greek civilizations were born.

Stone Age Triumph

The Ġgantija temple complex has two temples, north and south, which share a common façade and forecourt.

Today four of the largest temple complexes figure on the tourist trail. At least forty more survive in various stages of disarray. Others have disappeared completely, spirited away into boundary walls and house foundations. They were built on a small archipelago with a total land area of little more than three hundred square kilometres: a massive stone construction for every seven square kilometres. As archaeologist, Dr David Trump, has written: 'there is probably no other area of this size in the world with such a number and variety of antiquities'. The oldest and best preserved of the

Ġgantija

is the maltese word for giantess and folk stories refer to a female giant who carried the great slabs by day and built the temple by night.

temples is on Gozo, the second largest and most northerly of the islands. As with all their other temples the builders selected a choice site. Its great, grey mass stands on one of the island's distinctive flat-topped hills above a fertile valley. Its vast megaliths, never completely covered by the silting up of time, led to folk stories of a female giant who, by day, strode the land carrying the great slabs on her head, and built by night. It is still called Ġgantija, the Maltese word for giantess. The builders found on the islands an abundance of two kinds of limestone: a durable grey upper layer and beneath it one that cuts and looks like butter. They put both to good use in nearly all of their temples but nowhere else did they build a surrounding wall quite as astonishing as the one at Ġgantija. Massive blocks of hard grey stone, one of them the size of a small cottage, are laid alternately upright and sideways to form a first course eight metres high. Above them smaller blocks teeter

An aerial view of the main temple of Ħaġar Qim.

upwards for a further two metres. Two temples, with great lobed chambers, built of smaller stones, share this colossal overcoat. The two entrances stand side by side on the concave façade, flanked by pillars of soft, golden limestone once doubtless capped by lintels of equally impressive dimensions. The oldest temple has a threshold made of one enormous slab of golden stone and beside it lie round rocks, the size of cannon balls, that rolled it into place. The interior walls were originally plastered and painted with red ochre, the remains of which could still be seen clinging to the stones until only a few years ago.

Stone altars, a fire-reddened circular stone hearth, libation holes, and a possible oracle hole give some indication of the ceremonies that were performed there. A keen eye can still see traces of typical temple carving, spirals and a simple but effective stippling of incised dots, on the soft stone surfaces.

Unhappily, Ġgantija was the first of the temples to be uncovered. In the 1820s it was dug out (rather than excavated) by enthusiastic but untrained hands. Many treasures must have disappeared with the rubbish. A carved snake climbing a stone, another rather more phallic stone, and two finely modelled stone heads give some indication of what else might have been there. A charming piece of pottery, part of a bowl incised all round with two lines of birds in flight, is difficult to associate with the term Stone Age.

Two more temple complexes, Ħaġar Qim and Mnajdra, which stand within sight of each other above the southern cliffs of the main island of Malta, received only slightly better treatment. But it was here, at Ħaġar Qim, that were found the statues that have become a symbol of the temple culture. They are known as 'fat ladies', though whether they really are ladies is still in dispute. They have massive hips, thighs and upper arms, and neat little hands and feet and sit in ladylike positions, but very few of them have female breasts. Most of them have detachable heads, which could be an argument either for or against.

Fortunately, Tarxien, the last great temple to be built, and the Hypogeum of Ħal Saflieni, an underground cemetry in use during almost the entire temple period, remained undisturbed until Malta had produced an archaeologist worthy of them. Both were discovered at the start of this century by builders digging foundations and both now stand in the middle of housing developments but at least most of their treasures were preserved. If there had ever been any doubt about the importance of the fat ladies in temple culture this was dispelled by the discovery of their giant sister at Tarxien. Local farmers, tired of catching her in their ploughs, had done their best to break her up, but her elegant feet, massive calves and out-size pleated skirt survived the onslaught. When complete she would have stood nearly

above: *A limestone statue found in 1839 during the excavation of Ħaġar Qim.*
left and bottom left: *This large statuette (39cm high) was discovered buried in a pit on the upper level of the Ħal Saflieni Hypogeum. It has traces of red pigment and a neck socket. Two heads were burried with it, only one of which fits the socket.*
bottom right: *A 7cm clay seated figure found during the Xagħra Circle excavations.*

A large stone spiral decorated screen found at Tarxien Central which is classified among the finest remains of Neolithic art.

three metres high. Placed on a richly carved plinth, and given the prime position, she was, breasts or no breasts, undoubtedly the deity – The Earth Mother, Life, the Goddess of Fertility, or whatever it was they called her. It had long been thought that animal sacrifice had played a part in temple rituals and Tarxien appears to have confirmed this. When the excavators removed a small flap, cut by the temple carvers into a richly decorated altar front, they found, in the cavity behind it, a long flint knife and a bundle of animal bones.

Tarxien displays the apex of the temple-carvers' art. As well as elaborate branched and running spirals, and the usual stippling, there are fine reliefs of bulls and horned sheep or goats and a sow followed by her piglets. A pair of particularly dense spirals stares sternly from a step leading up into what was probably the most sacred of the inner sanctums, like a pair of eyes keeping a watch for trespassers. The temple-

builders carved all this, as they did everything else from megaliths to underground caverns, with nothing to aid them but stone tools.

The Hypogeum, a man-made series of caves that reaches through several levels deep into the earth, is considered to be even more remarkable than the temples on the surface. An estimated seven thousand bodies were buried here, along with their grave goods of pottery, shells and polished stones, but the most astounding thing about it is the large circular chamber, cut from the living rock, to imitate the interior of the temples above ground. Many of the temples contained small models of themselves, but here, sheltered from the elements is a full-size replica unwithered by time.

What kind of people could they have been who created all these riches? Where did they come from and what happened to them?

Some of the answers are now emerging from another sub-terranean burial site,

A replica of the largest statue to be found in Malta's many neolithic temples and possibly the first colossal figure to be created anywhere in the world. When complete it would have stood at least 2.75 metres high. It was discovered in the south temple at Tarxien. The original is on display at the National Museum of Archaeology in Valletta.

the Brochtorff Circle, near Ġgantija on Gozo. An Anglo-Maltese team of archaeologists, meticulously probing and recording, has begun to piece the story together.

It seems that around 5000 BC the islands' first inhabitants made their way across the sea from Malta's nearest neighbour, Sicily, 90 kilometres to the north. They were farmers, growing barley and wheat and bringing with them cattle, goats, sheep and pigs. They appear to have been a remarkably peaceful people, fearing no threat from each other or from the outside world. They lived in caves and mud-brick houses without a trace of any kind of fortification. The only things found from this period even resembling a weapon are two tiny arrowheads.

They also appear to have been unusually healthy with strong bones and teeth. Rather touchingly a few of them had bunions and one small child was buried with a puppy. It could be that only the privileged few were

buried here but several skeletons seem to indicate otherwise. These were men with particularly thick, strong limbs and distinctively craggy faces. It is tempting to think that they were the ones who moved the megaliths.

The same team tentatively put forward a theory which might explain the whole temple phenomenon. It begins with the islands themselves, which are rich in clay, stone and sunshine, and usually, though not always, in winter, rain. In summer the land bakes dry. There are springs but no rivers and even in the valleys the soil level is thin. Trees barely figure in the landscape now and, it seems, there were scarcely more when the temple-builders first

arrived. It was a land uninhabitable until men had learned to farm. Over the centuries, to make room for more agriculture, the hillsides have been terraced with dry-stone walls and it may well have been the temple builders who constructed the first of them.

For a thousand years or more the new settlers seem to have maintained links with the outside world. They had tools of flint and obsidian, which could never have been available on Malta itself, and the tiny greenstone axes that were common exchange goods of the time. Their pottery remained similar to that on Sicily and the mainland of Southern Italy. Then a distinctive local culture began to emerge. The pottery changed

83

completely, unique bone pendants were made, of a shape found nowhere else, and local chert began to be used instead of the superior imported flint and obsidian. It was at this stage that the first temples were built. As the temple culture flourished, the temples themselves appear to have become the guardians of what remained of these now rare, imported goods.

The thinking is that, as the islands became increasingly isolated, the rivalry and prestige involved in foreign trade was transferred to the building of great monuments. As the population grew, every settlement not only had to have one of its own, but one bigger and better than all the rest. It is an idea that brings a wry smile to the lips of present day Maltese as they look about them and see cathedral-sized church domes rising from every town and village. Until recently it was assumed that the temple builders, after their last fine flourish at Tarxien, had been replaced by a very different race, who brought with them tools and weapons of copper and bronze. But there is now some evidence to show that the two cultures may have overlapped and that not all

the temple builders were driven off the islands. It would be pleasant to think that Malta's modern building skills were a talent inherited from such remarkable ancestors.

It's FIESTA season

This is a visitors detailed account on his recollections of a Maltese festa.

"I MUST SAY I HAD BEEN WARNED.

MY HOTEL RECEPTIONIST GAVE ME A TASTE OF WHAT TO EXPECT BY A RATHER DETAILED ACCOUNT OF HER OWN FATHER'S EXPLOITS AT HER OWN VILLAGE FESTA THE PREVIOUS WEEK.

And the coach driver who took us to the festa last night just kept flashing his tobacco-stained snigger in the rear-view mirror each time he overheard any of us say how much we were all looking forward to it all.

It was the smell that hit me first. More than the crowds, more than the lights, more than the generally chaotic wandering of a village community acting as if they had not seen each other for many years. Dazzling lights at the ends of short sticks sparkled into nowhere as children (loads of them) ran around through the gathering leaving behind trails of a beautiful whiff of gunpowder bouquet.

I looked up from where I was standing at one end of a typical village square, like so many I had seen on my trip to Malta. All around, ornate statues cast demeaning looks onto the crowd below from the equally ornate pedestals on which they had been placed. I didn't know who the statues represented, so I asked a distracted father standing next to me. He didn't know either but suggested they were saintly friends of the village's own patron saint.

I couldn't quite agree; none of them seemed to share the enthusiasm of the villagers' annual tribute to their protective overlord.

Straight ahead of me was the magnificent church, its weathered limestone glowing under a million coloured bulbs. I was told that volunteers spend a whole year preparing for the decorations which go up each time this time of the year. Collections are even held regularly during the year to fund this communal fling.

I shuffled my way through tons of small bits of paper strewn across the square to take a glimpse of the church's interior. The papers had been showered onto the patron saint's statue from crowded balconies and roofs as it was merrily paraded through the village's main streets earlier in the evening.

It did take a while for me to get to the church. On the way, burly vendors kept shouting 'nooga' at me until I realised that the antique weighing scales proudly crowning their intricate stands were lumbered with bars of delicious nougat. I sank my teeth into a crispy bit handed to me 'just to taste'. This is what I call direct marketing. For the rest of the evening, I dragged along a

bag of several types of nougat for my friends back home.

I was on the church parvis by now when I hear a loud bang. Feverishly, I look around but panic seemed to have struck nobody but myself. I realised a firework petard had gone off somewhere and thought I had missed a colourful display. There was none of the sort. Over the next couple of hours, petards would go off over the village every few minutes. Loud bangs but no colour. I thought I had been conned into believing all the hype about Maltese fireworks displays.

Away from the crowd, I silently crept round the church's aisle and side chapels. Red damask covered the inspiring colonnades around the church and the patron saint's statue rose proudly from a garden of flowers arranged all around the pedestal.

An ageing veiled woman stood up from her prayers and smiled at me. She explained that the Lord too wanted us mortals to rejoice at our saints' feasts

and that she was hurrying back to her home where her family awaited. She did however seem concerned that the village's youths viewed the festa more as a glorified beer drinking bout than an annual tribute to a watchful friend in need and in deed. She made a distinction between the *festi ta' barra* (outdoor festivities) and the *festi ta'gewwa* (indoor festivities). What went on outside was not directly organised by the church itself which was, of course, more concerned with the religious devotion and prayer associated with the festa. The usual appeals against too much drink and unruly behaviour in the piazza and village streets had gone out. Back out on the piazza I noted an impeccably-dressed middle-aged man shaking hands with every one who crossed his path. Or rather, he seemed to be intent on crossing the paths of everyone in the square to shake hands with them and give the occasional thump on their backs. I was told he was one of the local politicians and that the slightest hint of a lack of enthusiasm for the village feast could seriously affect his performance at the polls next time round. I realised, after all, it was not only our local constituency

politician back home who did this sort of thing.

By now the bustle was getting, well, getting worse so I decided to move away from the square and explore the quieter narrow alleys behind the church. All the homes seemed ablaze with light bulbs on racks laid across the carved wooden balconies. The doors to most houses were flung wide open and inside I could see whisky-pouring fathers entertaining friends, family or anyone who bothered to listen to their anecdotes on their alcohol induced antics at last year's festa. In some homes, I could see plastic sofa covers neatly tucked away beneath the staircase. The village festa must truly be an important occasion.

Back into the square and a certain commotion arose. Someone lit a small petard at the end of a long stick and what followed was a half-hour display of fireworks on the ground, the likes of which I had never seen before. Catherine wheels revolved on rickety poles showering fiery trails in lunatic circles. One of them had nine spinning wheels each simultaneously turning in opposing directions. The crowd clapped as each one of the dozen or so spinning wheels lit up and burnt its way through the memory of those watching.

A crowd of sweaty young men, dressed only in shorts, some even barefooted, got together like a rugby scrum; arms placed on the shoulders of the next one, jumping into the air and shouting *viva l-festa taghna*. They aimlessly bulldozed their way to the nearest bar and re-emerged with the equivalent of a vat of beer in small brown bottles. And it was *viva l-festa taghna* all over again as the village band struck up its merry tunes once again. Shy young ladies dressed in their festa best marched besides their lovers playing in the band, occasionally stealing from them a loving glance away from the beer-stained music notes perched precariously over their shining wind instruments. One dragged a huge bass drum on an antique pram.

Then all eyes shot up into the clear night sky. Trails of silvery fire traced their way across the black darkness of infinity above; umbrella streaks of colours which would have baffled even Newton in his studies on the spectrum. I had never seen anything like it. Fireworks factories dot the Maltese countryside and I could now see why so many of them are around. One village festa could have as much as three such factories working right through the year for this hour-long spectacle of light, colour and, of course, devotion.

I craned my neck to get a better view and between the church's dome and bell towers there unfolded the most beautiful spectacle I had ever seen before. The fireworks in the sky over, a deafening noise shot out in the dark from above the band club headquarters in the square. I turned around, and the *kaxxa infernali* was like the Royal Navy gone mad. Loud bursts of noise and white light shot above the club roof's parapet in riotous spurts up to what seemed like a thousand a second. These fireworks from hell, which is what they are called in Maltese, must indeed make hell a scary place even for its keepers if they really exist down there. I turned to leave and walked away from the square. I had been warned, but nothing can really describe the unforgettable evening I had spent. From the heavenly embrace of touching devotion to the hellish sound of rocketing petards, the village festa had brought the best out of the Malta I had by then come to known. Colour, tradition, noise and, above all, the smiles all around.

In a quaint street not far from the church, I crossed paths with the old lady I had spoken to inside the church. She looked at me and smiled again. Her veil was off this time and she sheepishly invited me to join her family for a drink with the words:

VIVA L-FESTA TAGHNA".

Olive oil in

Roman times

It is unclear whether the olive was known to the people of Malta before the arrival of the Romans, but it is more than likely that it was. The islands were, at the time of the take-over by Rome in 218 BC, colonized by the Carthaginians – and the olive was a staple product of that North African city Carthage. For many centuries it was an important crop for the Carthaginians' Phoenician ancestors in the Near East. The olive presses found in Malta and Gozo all date to the Roman period, and there are enough to show that olive oil production was plentiful and something on which the people depended. The olives to feed these presses must have come from substantial groves. Olive-picking is labour intensive and the declining financial rewards, with increased competition all over the Mediterranean area, probably led to the eventual abandonment and destruction of the groves. Maltese place-names, however, testify to the popularity of the olive.

Village names Żebbuġ, which means olive, and Żejtun, which is an ancient name for a particular type of oil-yielding olive, are just two.

Olive presses were found during the excavation of rustic villas. A distinction must be made however between the three main types of Roman dwelling remains found in Malta and Gozo: the 'farm' villa, the holiday villa, and the townhouse, or domus. The dwelling at Rabat, which is generally known as the Roman Villa, is a typical domus and not a villa. It stood in what was then a thriving city, Melita.

The holiday villa was a home away from home for wealthy families. Remains of these, complete with baths

and mosaics, have been found in the Għajn Tuffieħa area to the north of Malta, and on the beach at Ramla l-Ħamra in Gozo. Remains of 'farm' villas are far more common and have been uncovered scattered in fertile areas all over Malta, but particularly in the Rabat area. These were plain and simple houses and would have provided shelter to families who worked the land.

Olive pressing formed just a part of the agricultural way of life which involved farming and herding. Self-sufficiency was then the ultimate goal and often the only way to survive. People who lived a rustic life away from the town centres did their best to produce everything they needed on their own estates, venturing into the city only when they had surplus produce to sell, or some exceptional requirement to buy. A villa would have had its own olive press in much the same way as each house might now have a refrigerator or a washing-machine. These families grew the olives, picked them, and processed them into the staple olive oil, which was then kept in vast pottery vessels in a cool part of the house. In most instances, excavations have revealed nothing but the foundations and heavy olive presses, the presses having survived the passage of the years because they are generally too heavy and unwieldy to remove without the help of machinery. House stones were often removed for re-use, but the same could not be done with the presses, as they became redundant when the olive supply dried up. These presses were removed to museums and the foundations surveyed and covered up. The areas in which these remains were found are, by and large, still agricultural. One press was found in a valley at Bidnija, a rural area known for its vegetable production. It stood among a few ancient olive trees which are still standing. Though the press is much older than they are, the continuity is evident. Another olive press was found during excavations in the same area, within the remains of a large rustic villa at San Pawl Milqi at Burmarrad.

The olives of Malta are not mentioned in the ancient literary sources; these speak only of textiles. The evidence we have is entirely from the archaeological record. Ovid, in a poem, contrasted the fertility of Malta to the sterility of Pantalleria.

A house without olive oil was like a house without soap or bread. It was used not only in the preparation of food but to cleanse the body. In the *unctoria* of public baths, bathers were rubbed with olive oil after their various hot and cold plunges. The bather, if he could afford the expense, was anointed before, after, and during the bathing process. The wealthy used a slave to carry the oil-bottles (*ampulla olearia*) and scraper (*strigilis*), with which the oil and perspiration were removed from the skin. The truly wealthy

used the perfumed oils of the Near East.

Olives were hugely popular on the Italian peninsula, which Varro referred to as "one large orchard". Vast *latifundia*, some of them the size of the Maltese islands, were worked by slaves for the production of enormous quantities of agricultural goods, including olive oil. *Venafrum, Casinum* and the Sabine country were celebrated for their oils. The typical Roman breakfast *(ientaculum)* is recorded as having been bread, dipped in wine or flavoured with salt, grapes, olives, cheese or eggs.

The remains at Pompeii give a good indication of what a Roman oil-and-olives shop looked like. Such shops were essential in the town where the residents did not produce their own oil. In the street leading towards the Odeum, there is the shop of an oil merchant, with eight earthenware vessels let into the counter, in which olives and clotted oil were found.

The olive plays its part in the Maltese diet, but obviously, is no longer used for bathing purposes. Bread drizzled with olive oil remains a staple food, though it is now flavoured with tomatoes, which were unknown to the Romans, having been introduced from the Americas long after Rome declined and fell.

Malta is well on the way to becoming a fully-fledged olive oil producing nation once more. More than 150,000 imported olive tress have been planted in recent years. The ultimate aim is to have many groves of indigenous olive trees, which would render a true Maltese olive oil. Olive oil produced locally is by nature fruity, pungent and full of taste, all the characteristics of true extra virgin olive oil.

Hidden **charms**

Many houses are being restored, often as family homes, and unfortunately many architectural details are being covered up or removed.

A peculiarity that has been eliminated from most older houses and farmhouses is what the locals called the *mirkeb* (meaning 'to go onto from'). It consists of two or three steps on the façade, the lowest step being at street level situated on the left as one comes out of the main door of the house. Also on the façade but about one metre above ground level, was a stone with a hole in its centre, called *marbat* (meaning 'to tie with'). Many wonder what use these steps, seemingly leading to nowhere, could have been.

A careful look at the façade of old farmhouses, can reveal certain details in the architecture that may go by unnoticed.

Before cars became so popular, most houses and farmhouses had a donkey, mule or horse-drawn cart. The beast was taken out of its stable and tied to the *marbat*. Others even had a small 'garage' for the wooden cart.
The cart was taken out and attached

The stone supports seen below windows had varied uses: they were used for drying cheese or, if a potted plant placed on one of the supports, it signified that a girl of marriageable age lived there.

to the beast. The load was then placed on the cart, the 'driver' untied the animal and would mount the cart via the three steps.

Since the motor-car was introduced during the British colonial period, driving has always been on the left. However, before the arrival of the British in 1800, driving of carts was on the right of the roads. The *mirkeb* steps are built in such a way that the driver 'boards' on the left side of the cart. Nowadays, although carts observe left-hand driving, most farmers still sit on the left side of the cart, a clear reminiscent of past practice. Since many roads have been paved these steps regrettably, have been systematically removed.

The stone slab with the hole, the *marbat*, can still be seen on the façades of many houses. As all households had a donkey, mule or horse, this was where the animal was tied before it was led to the stable. The *marbat* is sometimes in the form of a metal ring hammered into the wall. Curiously, farmers sometimes hammered the metal head of the local plough into the wall, leaving the space where the wooden handle normally is, jutting out of the wall. The rope was tied to this. Some houses, especially in the villages, were built in such a way that a well was dug in the foundations of the building. The household could get water from openings that led directly to the well from various rooms in the house. The well's main head with the traditional *horża* covering it, was in the

central courtyard or garden. Some houses also had a wellhead with a trough in the façade, which served to quench the thirst of the beast of burden on hot summer days. If water had to be carried off somewhere in containers, these were placed on the cart and filled from this wellhead . Most of these façade wellheads have now been blocked off.

A curious feature in some façades usually found close to the main or kitchen doorway, about half a metre above ground, is yet another hole, 15 by 15 centimetres. From the outside, the hole leads straight into the wall, turns sideways and then straight out the other side. This is the cat's hole. Being well above ground, it prevented rodents from sneaking into the house, but a cat could jump up and wriggle through.

Hearsay has it that this hole was also condidered a form of protection against burglars. Thieves often tricked housewives into opening the door for them by scratching on the door, pretending to be the household cat asking to come in. Since the cat had its hole to come and go as it pleased, it did not need to scratch on the door, and a thief seeing the hole would know that his common trick would not work.

Another feature found in the façade of some houses is the spy or peep-hole. Houses that had a stone balcony usually had decorated holes in the form of a crescent moon, stars, the eight-pointed cross of the knights of Malta, flowers, or other shapes in the stonework. One could look through these holes and see whoever was on the street below without being seen. For houses without a balcony, another form of spyhole was inserted under a window sill. The façade was cut in such a way that somebody standing inside the window had a peephole to look through and could see who was knocking at the door of the house. Another peculiar detail is the presence of two supports on either side of a window protruding onto the façade, yet supporting nothing. Between these supports, a shelf was normally inserted on which the local homemade cheese and other foods were dried. The shelf was built of a thin slab of stone or a plank of wood.

These supports had another use too. A potted plant placed on one of the supports signified that a girl of marriageable age lived there. Gentlemen were expected to come forward and ask for the hand of the girl. Lastly, if one looks at the top of many older houses, it is common to see a series of small holes. These served as pigeon holes, known as *barumbara*, where birds could seek shelter and perhaps lay their eggs. This was a common sight in many houses, since pigeons were inexpensive to keep and pigeon broth and roasted pigeon were favourite Maltese dishes.

Naxxar Opulence

An outstanding and rare example of Maltese extravagance; this family house is drear
owners whose principal residence in Valletta adjoining the Auberge de Castille i
1798 when he evicted the Order of St John and made Malta a French territory. Palazz
the architectural intervention and lavish attention to detail of the renowned banke

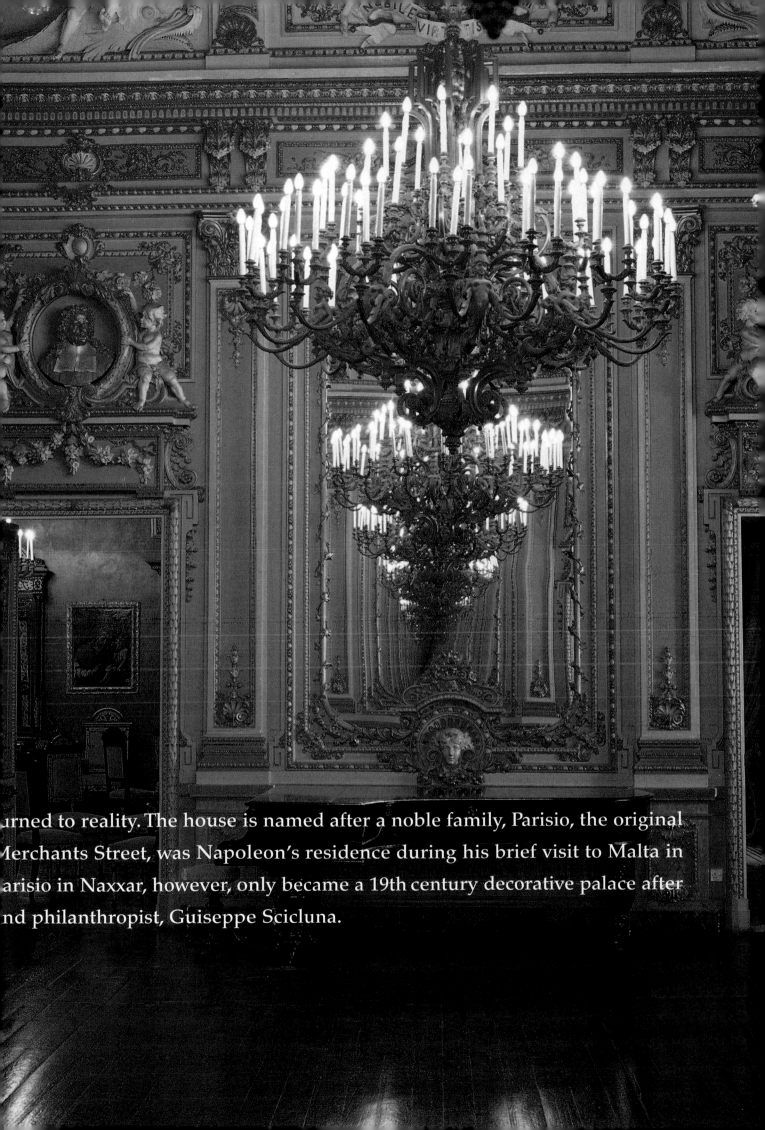

urned to reality. The house is named after a noble family, Parisio, the original
Merchants Street, was Napoleon's residence during his brief visit to Malta in
arisio in Naxxar, however, only became a 19th century decorative palace after
nd philanthropist, Guiseppe Scicluna.

When Pope Piux IX created Giuseppe
Scicluna a marquis, his reputation as a
philanthropist was well established.
Towards the end of the 19th century,
his magnificent bank in Valletta
(destroyed in World War II) and his
delightful Dragonara Palace (whose
gate bears the memorable Latin legend
'God made this haven for us') which is
now the Dragonara Casino, would be
joined by the greatest Scicluna edifice
of all, Palazzo Parisio in Naxxar.
The great works were started in 1898
and were only completed about a year
before Giuseppe died in 1907. The
result was astonishing. The rebuilding
stretched local and Italian artisans to
the extreme of their abilities.
Decorators led by the Italian Carlo
Sada and his team set new standards
for Malta: the gilded hall of mirrors;
the Pompeiian embellishments; the
extensive use of marble; and then, the
Italian artist Filippo Venuti, who had
exhibited his work in Rome, Turin and
Paris painted the allegories.
The marble at Palazzo Parisio is
remarkable too: no small tiles
anywhere, everything is vast. It would
be a pity to visit the place and not to
take careful note of the great coping
stone over the balustrade leading to
the upper floor. It is the longest single
piece of marble on the islands, and
the romance of it all – how it was
transported by countless mules – is a
legend not to be forgotten in the
history of the building of Malta.
www.palazzoparisio.com

The gardens at Palazzo Parisio are a surprise, formally Italianate and decorative in two great garden enclosures. Once an old path lead all the way to San Pawl ta' rga with a belvedere overlooking a breath-taking view towards St Pa islands.

A third generation of heirs has restored this great heirloom to its former dignity, a unique Maltese palazzo open to the public.

La Sacra **Infermeria**

*THE ILLUSTRIOUS MEDITERRANEAN CONFERENCE CENTRE WAS ONCE
THE HOLY INFIRMARY OF THE KNIGHTS OF THE ORDER OF ST JOHN*

The Mediterranean Conference
Centre in Valletta is impressive by any
standards. Behind its plain façade lie
great halls, wide staircases and
treasures dating back to 1580. It is
architecturally superb. Little wonder
its restoration and conservation won
the Europa Nostra Award.

Of course today it has been adapted
to the needs of modern enterprise.
Large international conferences are held
here, so too are trade fairs. Its theatre is
also the venue for grand scale operas,
ballets and musicals, many of them
presented by companies visiting
from Europe.

The functional title of Conference
Centre obscures the fact that this is a
stunning place.

After the Great Siege in 1565, the
Order of St John set about rebuilding
and fortifying the Islands. They had been
based in Birgu (Vittoriosa) but, seeing
the benefits of the strategic ground
where Valletta stands now decided to
build a new city there. They called it

107

Valletta in honour of Grand Master Jean Parisot de la Valette who led them to victory against the Turks during the siege.

By 1574 Valletta had begun to take shape and they laid the foundation stones for the new Knights' hospital outside Fort St Elmo. Originally the Sacra Infermeria, the Holy Hospital, was built around a courtyard with two wards and a series of small rooms. By 1580 more wards were added and, George Sandys, son of the Archbishop of York wrote in 1610 that the infirmary merits "regard not only for the building but for the entertainment (care) there given. Served they [the sick] are by junior knights on silver".

Between 1660 and 1680 two Grand Masters, the brothers Raphael and Nicholas Cottoner, undertook further expansion of the hospital and created the Great Ward – later renamed the Long Ward.

At 155 metres long, 11 metres wide and more than 11 metres high was the longest ward in Europe. Its wooden ceiling was considered the finest example of timber construction. Along the walls were niches at ground level

which served as latrines for the sick. During the winter tapestries were hung from the walls; during the summer these were replaced with paintings. Beneath the Long Ward and reached by a grand balustraded staircase is the *Sala del Magazzena Grande*, the Great Magazine Ward, with its superbly cross-vaulted ceiling and heraldic bosses where the groins meet. Extensive additions were made to the hospital in 1712 including a pharmacy, laboratory, residential quarters for medical staff and a small chapel. Over the chapel doorway is the Latin inscription *Cum Percussi Aspicient Sanabunter Num* – whosoever being struck shall look upon it and live – a reference to the bronze serpent erected by Moses so that Israelites bitten by serpents in the desert could look upon it and be healed. The patients in the Infirmary were both Maltese and foreign with

special concern given to Catholics. The needy and infirm, like children, were all welcomed.

The hospital rules were always carefully applied. Wards were meticulously clean and airy; any patients found playing dice or cards, or being noisy, were expelled.

Food was served to the patients on silver platters with silver spoons.

This was not so much as to honour the patients, or show the wealth of the Order, but for health reasons. Silver could be easily cleaned and was considered not to harbour germs. When Napoleon threw the knights out of Malta in 1798 he ordered all the silver to be auctioned in order to pay his soldiers wages and fund his navy. When the British forces took over in

September 1800 having supported the Maltese uprising against the French, they filled the Sacra Infermeria with ailing British troops and renamed the building the Garrison Hospital. Fifty years later substantial alterations were made, all with the intention of allowing more air and light into the wards. The closets built into the recesses in the walls were removed and lavatories were built outside the wards.

By the beginning of World War I the hospital's patients numbered less than 100 and many small wards were closed. But with the troop landings at Gallipoli on April 25, 1915 and the great numbers of casualties this caused, the Garrison Hospital expanded again as it became the largest of the hospitals in Malta to receive the wounded. Malta became known as the Nurse of the Mediterranean. Hospital ships ferried the seriously ill from Gallipoli to the Grand Harbour where they were brought ashore. Numbers were so high that all the wards, now reopened after years of neglect, were seriously overcrowded. As soon as hostilities ceased, decision was taken to build larger hospitals that would service the future needs of the growing population and garrison.

It is no longer possible when touring the building to see all the details envisioned by the Order of St John: where mothers could

abandon their unwanted babies, where syphilis was treated with mercury injections, or the various private rooms reserved for infectious diseases or where the Knights themselves were treated. The alterations and improvements made by the British Forces during their reign and the damage caused in World War II removed these. But the building itself is nonetheless rewarding. Much remains and every stone seems to tell a story.

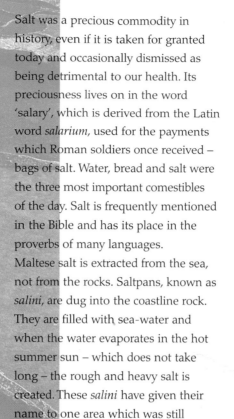

Salt was a precious commodity in history, even if it is taken for granted today and occasionally dismissed as being detrimental to our health. Its preciousness lives on in the word 'salary', which is derived from the Latin word *salarium,* used for the payments which Roman soldiers once received – bags of salt. Water, bread and salt were the three most important comestibles of the day. Salt is frequently mentioned in the Bible and has its place in the proverbs of many languages.

Maltese salt is extracted from the sea, not from the rocks. Saltpans, known as *salini,* are dug into the coastline rock. They are filled with sea-water and when the water evaporates in the hot summer sun – which does not take long – the rough and heavy salt is created. These *salini* have given their name to one area which was still

Some of the earliest known saltpans are those of Xwieni in Gozo. They are said to date back to the Roman period and are cut into a shelf of soft limestone which runs along the water's edge. This area is now a chequerboard of shallow pits, some of them with edges reinforced now with large cemented pebbles. The *salini* here stretch for around one kilometre.

The Xwieni saltpans are labour-saving in that they are filled by wave action, and not by buckets – though this does not happen in the calm hot weather. Canals hewn into the rock distribute the water to the remoter saltpans, and the salt-harvesters have gouged out deep holes which reach the sea level, enabling them to haul it up as though from a well. When the salt is dry it is then lifted and commercially cleaned and packed. This is perhaps the most

The Xwieni salt pans in Gozo date back to the Roman period and have been in regular use for over two thousand years producing A harvest of **Salt**

used for salt production until fairly recently, Salina Bay. The old ramshackle wooden shacks where the salt-gathering equipment was housed, are still standing there today.

Perhaps this salt-gathering is the legacy of colonial Rome. The Romans were masters at producing salt. Salt from the harbour town of Ostia was carried along the Via Salaria (the 'salt highway') to Rome and other parts of Italy.

remarkable aspect of these beautifully constructed saltpans: they have been in regular use for some two thousand years.

The Xwieni *salini* are the most remarkable in the Maltese islands. Smaller stretches of pans exist in other areas, but they are not as impressive. Time and the relentless action of the winter waves have eroded many of the pans which created an ancient industry.

The Castle on a Hill

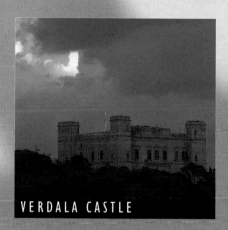

VERDALA CASTLE

in seven acres of gardens overlooking the wooded area of Buskett, takes its name from the Grand Master by whose order it was built in 1586, Hughes Loubenx de Verdalle. It is not so much a castle as a fortified country villa, and was both a place of repose and a hunting lodge.

Ugone de Loubenx delli Sig.ri Verdala essendo d'anni 16 fatte le prove di sua nobilta`è ricevuto per fratello della Milizia di S.Giovanni Geros.mo nella Vener. lingua di Provenza, vien cinto col cingolo ed abito della sud.a Mil: l'anno 1546.

Verdala essendo Governatore dell'Artiglieria ac e risarcisce gli strumenti di guerra, e si diporta i sta carica con universale soddisfazione l'anno

This grand house, which is surrounded by a dry ditch crossed by a bridge, is built on a near-symmetrical scale, with a basement and two other floors bound in by bastioned corner towers. Tradition attributes its design to the noted Maltese architect Gerolamo Cassar, but certain features are not typical of his known work. The balustraded parapet above the main cornice is an 18th century addition. Verdala Castle was never intended to serve as a stronghold although it looks like one. The roof is strong enough to take the weight of pieces of artillery, but the walls are thin by comparison, and with many apertures. The most it could have offered in the way of security was the fending off of small raiding parties of corsairs.

Three carriage gates, opening on to Zebbug Road, Mdina Road and Boschetto Road, lead into the grounds.

The Mdina Road gate bears the coat-of-arms of Grand Master Lascaris (1636–1657). Another archway, which

...a amministrando in convento molte e principali con somma diligenza e intiera fedeltà, viene ...vitore e procuratore, del comun tesoro per Tolosa

Verdala essendo Commen.ᵉ vien eletto Ambasciadore ordinario della S.ᵗᵃ Rel. Ger al S. Pontefice Greg.ⁱᵒ XIII. In questo mentre gli si conferisce dal Seren.ᵐᵒ Consi- glio la dignità di Gran Commendatore. L'anno del Signore 1570

leads into the courtyard, bears the arms of Grand Master Nicholas Cotoner (1663–1680). This quadrangular courtyard housed stables for 30 horses, together with their carriages, adjacent to the servants' quarters.

WORKS OF ART

The vaulted ceiling of the area known as 'the dining-room' is decorated with the coats-of-arms of the Grand Masters Pinto and de Verdalle. Frescoes on the walls represent War, Religion, Peace and the Order of St John. A large fresco shows de Verdalle as Grand Master. There are also two large canvasses: *Taurus Tormented by the Spirits*, by P P Caruana, and *Ajax Escaping from the Tempest*, by S Busuttil. In this great hall, the vaulted ceiling carries depictions of mythical figures, including Flora, Pallas, Bacchus and Mars. These have only recently been recovered from an overlay of paint which disguised them for years. They were painted over on the orders of the wife of one British governor in

117

the 1930s, who had taken a dislike to their apparent lack of decorum. A series of frescoes portrays the foremost events in the life of de Verdalle: his reception into the Order of St John, his promotion to Governor of Artillery, his role as Receiver and Procurator for the Priory of Toulouse, his ambassadorship to the Holy See, his receiving of the Grand Cross, his appointment as Grand Master, his elevation to Cardinal and his formal induction into the College of Cardinals by Pope Sixtus V. These frescoes are the late 16th century work of the Florentine Filippo Paladini and were restored in 1853.

Two 19th century frescoes show the British Governor Reid with a background of Verdala Castle on which the British flag flies, and a view of the Grand Harbour. Other paintings include *Jacob's Dream* and *The Disobedient Prophet*. The drawing-room's vaulted ceiling bears other Paladini frescoes which also glorify de Verdalle.

In the main hall on the upper storey, there are works of art which various Grand Masters commissioned to depict their material achievements. Shown here are the palazzo in which Grand Master Pinto lived, the Auberge de Castille and Fort Manoel. There are also portraits, including those of the Grand Masters Vilhena, Ximenes, Hompesch, and that of an unknown Cardinal. A painting showing a witch, which hangs in one of the bedrooms on this floor, is the work of the well-known Maltese artist, Edward Caruana Dingli.

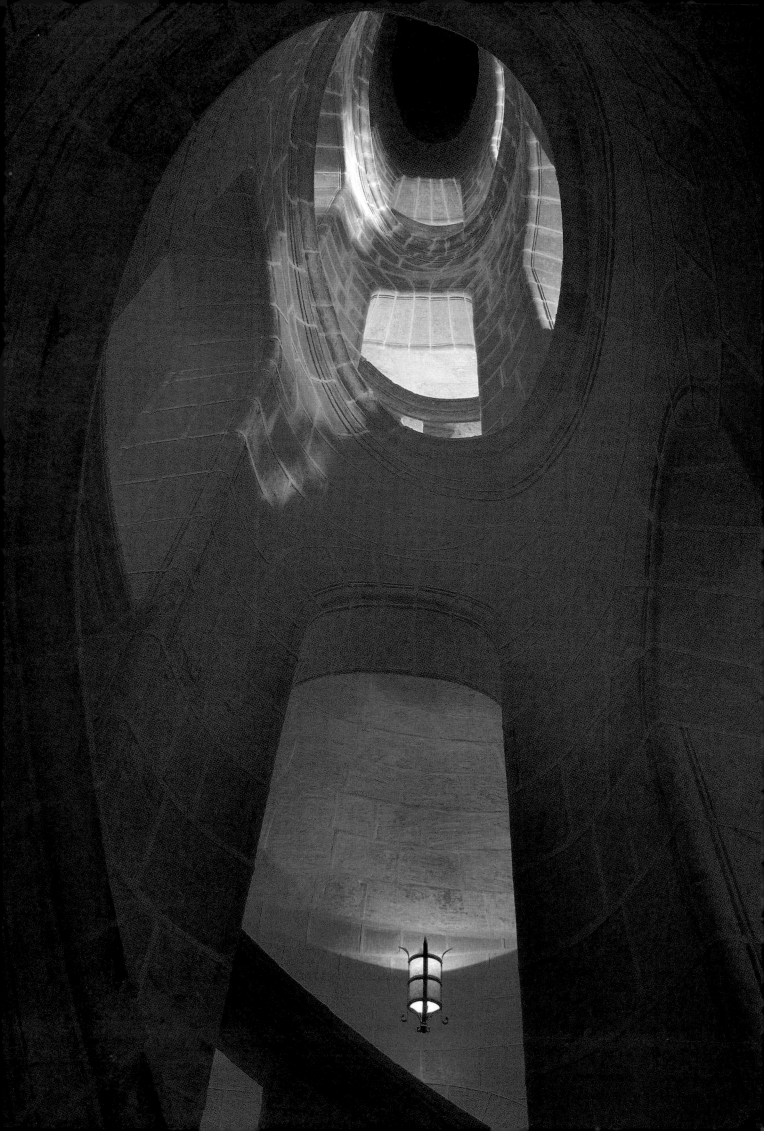

THE RESIDENT GHOST No noble home would be complete without a haunting presence. Verdala Castle's own ghost is the Blue Lady who is said to appear at a tower window, on the terrace, and in one of the guest rooms. In recent times she has been conspicuous by her absence.

THE BLUE LADY is reputed to be Cecile, a niece of the Grand Master de Rohan. She was the daughter of his sister who disgraced the family by eloping with a commoner, and she found herself in her uncle's care. It is said that after his death, during the time of the French occupation of Malta, her fiancé was tortured so as to be made to divulge the whereabouts of a supposed treasure hoard at Verdala Castle. Cecile took hold of the sword of a French soldier, killed her fiancé to end his misery, and then jumped to her death from a castle window.

A TORTURE CHAMBER was discovered, in the late 19th century, in the thickness of the castle walls. The positions where prisoners were chained to the wall are still visible. There is also a man-sized hole in which, it is said, captives were buried alive if they refused to comply with their captors' requests. The castle basement was used as sleeping quarters for the servants, kitchens and storerooms. A tight spiral staircase, behind an inconspicuous door, leads directly to the apartments once occupied by the Grand Masters, and was possibly a secret exit.

THE CHAPEL was added to the castle by Grand Master Nicholas de Cotoner in the late 17th century. It is small and simple, and the columns which support the altar are decorated with carvings of the cotton plant, taken from the Cotoner coat-of-arms. There is a titular painting by Mattia Preti which shows St John the Baptist and St Anthony the Abbot kneeling before the Virgin Mary and Jesus. Two oval paintings, also by Preti, show St Raphael and St Nicholas.

The discerning visitor from Europe cannot help but notice that architecture in these islands has something familiar about it, even though many of its facets do not. The familiarities might be in the Baroque elements of our monumental architecture: the palazzi of Italy have similar façades. The churches too resemble those of Spanish America. But there is certainly 'that indefinable something'.

The differences are less subtle. The honey coloured stone, the flat roofs and, yes, most of all the ubiquitous enclosed balconies. They are literally everywhere, in all materials, shapes, colours and sizes. Where do they come from? Are they Sicilian or Spanish? Moorish or Arabic? Is their origin in Malta, like its language, due to the island's Semitic origins, or are the balconies the progeny of a more recent influence?

These are familiar questions frequently encountered. The answers, alas, are more like strangers, and hardly ever seen. These are some possible solutions.

Gallarija Maltija
The evolution of the enclosed Maltese balcony

The origins are unlikely to be directly Arab or Moorish. Although these islands boast of the most ancient edifices still standing, it does not appear there are any remaining from the Arab period of our history, which dates from the 9th to the 11th century. So where does the *gallarija* come from? The influence is undoubtedly Arabic, but is unlikely to have come to Malta directly, that is without passing first through some other influence.

It is believed the original balconies in Malta were not balconies at all, but 'machicolations' or bottomless balconies erected above the main gate on the façade of fortifications to discourage attacks on this vital point. Castles erected in the eastern Mediterranean around the 11th and 12th centuries were enhanced by these strange constructions, a fashion which was later copied in numerous fortifications in Europe itself.

In Malta, several buildings may today be seen with machicolations. The twin towers at San Pawl tat-Tarġa and the octagonal tower at Siġġiewi are perfect examples of this. The Torri Gauci at San Pawl tat-Tarġa has the machicolations closed off at the base, so that they now serve as balconies, albeit crude ones. The central corbels conceal human faces perpetually looking out for the enemy. The earliest balconies were no doubt made exclusively of stone. It is the one abundanant raw material. Timber had long since disappeared, as on other Mediterranean islands, to make ships. Iron had to be imported, and anyway needed timber or coal to be worked. Malta's master masons were very familiar with their soft limestone, and could do marvellous things with it. Under their skilful hands the straight stone slabs evolved into beautiful curvaceous, ornately carved balconies. The carving includes motifs such as the Maltese cross, the Saracen six-petalled flower, the French or Florentine fleur-de-lys, and many other subjects, concealing at the same time in their folds a number of 'peep' holes. These holes permit the occupant to look into the street without being seen, an essential and recurring theme in the construction of balconies and which indicate a clear connection with the *masharabiya* of the Arab and Persian world.

As Malta prospered under the knights the pressure on space in built up areas became a consideration. The balustrade of the stone balcony was soon found to occupy too much space on the balcony platform. The obvious solution was to make the wall thinner. This could not easily be done without some danger of the stone elements falling into the street below. The answer lay in changing the material used to wrought iron. By this time there were many shipwrights and other craftsmen in these islands. There was regular contact with Sicily and the Italian mainland and it was comparatively simple, if more expensive, to construct the balustrade in this material. In Naxxar,

particularly, one finds some beautiful simple and also imaginative ironwork, but one finds this approach to the space problem has been adopted in every town and village.

A later development in the evolution of the balcony again resulted from the problems of space. It was normal for the family that was marrying off their children, to have the new bride or groom living with the parents or in-laws. At some time this arrangement, as it no doubt would today, would be the cause of some friction and it would be necessary to delineate which parts of the communal home were to be used by which part of the family. This social development could be one of the factors contributing to the enclosure of the stone platform with timber. The result would be an extension of the room that lies within. A safe shelter from the sun, where little children could play, without coming to any harm. An observation post from which the ladies of the family could watch the world going by in the streets below. The variety of shapes depended first on the plan of the stone platform upon which the timber balcony was erected, so there were curved ones as well as

Balconies of wood, wrought iron and stone in varying shapes and sizes can be seen on most streets of Malta's capital city, Valletta.

rectangular. Nowadays, no one erects curved timber balconies. The cost of rectangular ones is already prohibitive, so it may be safely assumed curved balconies are generally older.

The timber balconies were usually fitted with louvred shutters, known in Maltese as *persjani* which could easily be an indication of their origin. The purpose was, of course, to allow the cool air in while at the same time prevent prying eyes from doing so. Similarly the occupants could easily look into the street below. Some balcony shutters are made so that the angle of the slats are adjustable. Originally in drab brown, later green, the timber balconies of the islands are now painted all the colours of the rainbow.

The story of the timber balcony does not end here. The observer will no doubt notice some have timber poles sticking out at right angles to the façade. This is usually in the poorer areas, where houses have been split up on a permanent basis, or knocked down and apartments erected. The residents have lost access to the roof or a garden and must therefore hang their washing out to dry in this fashion. A closer look at other balconies will uncover some other uses to which balconies have been put.

Some buildings, usually those occupied by the local agent of a shipping line or a consular office, will have a flag attached to a bracket on the side of a timber balcony. Other smaller brackets or lugs may be seen in the centre of the wooden panels that make up the façade of the balcony. These were used to hold a wrought iron bracket with a glass oil lamp at its extremity. They were put up and illuminated on festas, but have now been replaced by functional electric light bulbs.

The sides of some of the older timber balconies, particularly in lower parts of Valletta, have small sliding rectangular shutters, which together with some other contrivances, such as a hole in the stone floor, were designed to enable the occupant to see who was calling at the door.

131

Once upon a time

Does Malta have the oldest sundial in the world?

It seems that different cultures around the world were able to observe the seasonal changes of the sun's position in the sky, and its rising and setting on the horizon.

The days that seem to have mostly concerned these cultures were the first days of our four seasons: the winter solstice (22 December) when it is the shortest day, the summer solstice (21 June) when the day is the longest and the equinox days (21 March and 23 September) when day and night are equal.

The most widely known site is probably Stonehenge, in Avebury, England where its alignment with the sunrise of the summer solstice has been observed since 1740. Stonehenge is claimed to be not just a solar sun dial, but also a lunar and astrological observatory.

Many lesser known sites exist in other countries. In Europe Christian churches often have their axis orientated to conform with particular days of the year. A German prehistoric sanctuary –

that later became a chapel – at the rock formation of Die Externsteine, has a round window that lets the first sun's rays of the summer solstice shine onto the opposite wall.

The chambered mounds of New Grange, Knowth and Dowth in Ireland all have passages orientated to let the sun's rays enter. New Grange is in line with the sunrise of the winter solstice, Dowth the sunset of the same day, and the mound at Knowth has two inner passages, each in line with the equinox sunrise and sunset. Another chamber in Brittany, France, also has its passage orientated to receive the light of the winter solstice.

There are similar sites in Mexico. At Xochicalo, precisely at noon on the summer solstice, a sunbeam enters through the roof, forming a narrow streak of light. In Uaxactun three Maya pyramids appear to have been constructed to coincide with the sunrise of the four specific seasonal days. Another sundial has been observed

In 1891 Sir J Norman Lockyer discovered that the temple of Amon-Ra at Karnak, Egypt, had its main axis directed towards the sunset of the midsummer solstice. This, and later discoveries, led to the development of scientific astro-archaeology.

Many ruins around the world have been studied since, and it is surprising that a large number have similar alignments to the sun, moon and the stars.

main picture: **SUNRISE AT MNAJDRA**
inset: **THE TEMPLE OF AMON-RA AT KARNAK, EGYPT**

at Machu Pichu in Peru. In Chaco Canyon, New Mexico, an ancient sundial carved in the rock face marks the midday of the equinox and solstice days. The Big Horn Medicine Wheel, a stone circle in Wyoming, United States, was a place of summer solstice rituals. One of its spokes points to the sunrise of the summer solstice.

In Asia at Angor Wat, Cambodia, the main temple has its towers aligned with important days of the calendar. Similar alignments were also observed in many aboriginal ritual sites all over the world.

Studies have also been undertaken on the 30 odd prehistoric temples in Malta, considered to be the world's oldest free standing monuments. The most important of these are listed in the World Heritage Sites of UNESCO. From 1979 to 1982 a number of archeologists working on separate projects, studied the most important of these sites. Investigations proved inconclusive, but at one site they discovered what could prove to be the oldest sundial existing today.

Most of the prehistoric temples of Malta have their axis lined up towards east-south and west-south. Very few are aligned towards the north or the west, and one temple faces directly towards the east.

In the Qrendi district, close to the southern coastline cliffs, and just 450 metres west of the Neolithic temples of Ħaġar Qim, are the temples of Mnajdra, excavated in 1836. The Mnajdra site has two temples and the remains of a small one. Archaeologists refer to these three temples as Mnajdra I, II, III. In the morning of the equinox day, looking out of the main portal of Mnajdra I, the sun can be seen appearing over the hill and the sunlight enters the temple exactly parallel to the main axis of the building. Going into the main portal and looking inwards, the light illuminates the whole passage and the innermost altar.

Returning to the site every week, the beam of the sunrise becomes thinner as it passes through the main portal and enters the temple. As the sun on the horizon moves towards the south, the beam of light moves towards the north in the temple. When the sun reaches its most southerly position, on the winter solstice, the sunlight in the temple is now only a thin beam of light. Exactly at sunrise, a vertical megalithic stone

NEW GRANGE AND STONEHENGE ARE TWO OF THE BEST KNOWN EUROPEAN SITES WHERE ARCHITECTURE W DESIGNED TO ALIGN WITH THE SUN'S POSITION THROUGHOUT THE YEAR

NEW GRANGE, IRELAND

Roof box
Main entrance

Sunrise on winter sols

STONEHENGE, ENGLAND

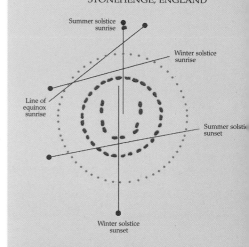

Summer solstice sunrise

Winter solstice sunrise

Line of equinox sunrise

Summer solstic sunset

Winter solstice sunset

IN THE AMERICAS, TOTALLY DIFFERENT PREHISTORIC CULTURES THAT SEEMINGLY HAD NO CONTACT WHATSOE WITH EUROPE OR ITS CIVILISATIONS, ALSO BUILT SITES ALIGNED TO THE SUN'S SEASONAL MOVEMENT.

UAXACTUM, MEXICO

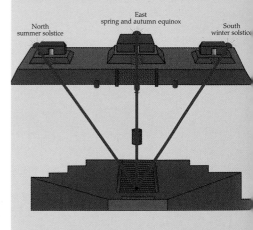

North summer solstice

East spring and autumn equinox

South winter solstic

BIG HORN MEDICINE WHEEL, WYOMING, US

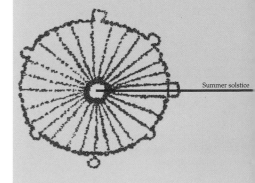

Summer solstice

Boulders

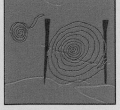

Winter solstice

Summer solstice

Equinoxes

IN CHACO CANYON, NEW MEXICO, ON A HILL JUTTING OUT OF THE DESERT AT THE ENTRANCE OF THE CANYON, ROLL BOULDERS HAVE BEEN PLACED ON A ROCK FACE IN SUCH A WAY THAT LIGHT 'DAGGERS' ARE FORMED AS THE MIDDAY SUNLIGHT PASSES THROUGH THE CRACKS BETWEEN THE BOULDERS. THE LIGHT 'DAGGERS' ON THE SOLSTICE AND EQUINOX DAYS HIT THE ROCK FACE ONTO TWO SPIRALS ENGRAVED INTO THE ROCK FACE.

inside the front 'room' is hit by the slit of light along its far edge. After the winter solstice the rising sun starts moving towards the north until it rises exactly in the east again on the equinox. When this movement of the sun happens, the beam in the temple starts to widen. It is widest on the day of the equinox, when again the main axis of the building is illuminated. Now the sun starts moving northwards, and again the beam of light starts to become thinner in the temple as it moves towards the south. As it reaches the most northerly position of the sun on the summer solstice, the beam of light reduces itself into a thin slit. Precisely as the rising sun appears over the hill this slit of light projects itself on another vertical megalithic slab, which is very similar to the stone that marks the winter solstice.

The beam of light of the summer solstice is much wider than the beam projected in the winter solstice. This could be because some of the stones forming the portal have eroded more than others, and so more light enters the building.

After the summer solstice, day-by-day, the beam starts moving towards the main passage of the building and reaches it on the next equinox day. This cycle must have occurred year after year since the building of this temple in about 3300 BC. The other sites discussed are all 'younger'. If it could be confirmed that this alignment was done intentionally, Malta could have the oldest sundial extant.

The evidence confirming this theory has increased. On the hill opposite Mnajdra a circular man-made hole was found in perfect alignment to where prehistoric man could have inserted a pole to mark the rising position of the winter solstice sunrise. If a similar hole was to be found on the northern side of the hill, in alignment with the sunrise of the summer solstice, then the alignment would most certainly be deliberately oriented.

A hole was found but it was off by three degrees, which would have made a big difference in the alignment of the temple. Perhaps this was only a tentative marker and the proper aligned marker-hole has yet to be found. (Provided of course, it has not been destroyed with the tilling of the fields.)

It is probable the temples were roofed and so the beam of light entering the temple would have been much brighter than nowadays. When the thin beam of light projects onto the vertical stone on the shortest day of the year, it is not at the very edge of the slab. Due to the sun's declination during the last 5,300 years, the beam of light has moved off the edge by about six centimetres. The equinox deplacement is nil and the summer solstice had its projection onto the very edge of the marker slab and lighted partly the niche behind the stone. Perhaps this was some kind of shrine connected with rituals celebrated on the longest day of the year.

Of course many historians wonder if

Mnajdra solar alignments

Flat stones
Vertical stones
Capstones
Fill

N

Winter solstice   Equinoxes   Summer solstice

BY NOTICING THE MOVEMENT OF THE RAY OF LIGHT ENTERING THE TEMPLE, OUR ANCESTORS COULD HAVE BUILT A SUNDIAL MARKING THE BEGINNING OF EVERY MONTH OF THE YEAR. IN THIS PHOTOGRAPHIC MULTIPLE EXPOSURE, USING AN ARTIFICIAL RAY OF LIGHT, AN EXAMPLE OF ALL THE MONTHLY MARKINGS IS SHOWN. THIS EXAMPLE WAS CARRIED OUT WITH AS MUCH PRECISION AS POSSIBLE. YET SINCE ARTIFICIAL LIGHT HAS FEWER PARALLEL LIGHT WAVES THAN SUNLIGHT, THE MARKINGS ARE NOT HITTING THE INSIDE OF THE TEMPLE MEGALITHS AS PRECISELY AS THE RISING SUN.

The sun retreats on its position at sunrise (and sunset) during the yearly 12 month cycle. On the June solstice it rises in the most east-north position on the horizon. On the equinoxes it rises exactly due east, and on the December solstice it rises the most east-south on the horizon.

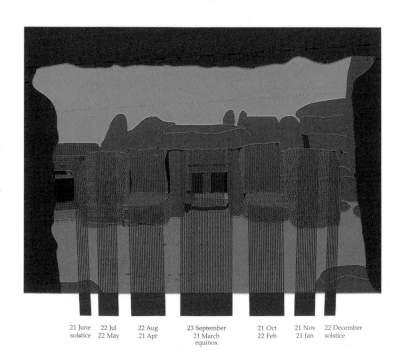

21 June solstice · 22 Jul 22 May · 22 Aug 21 Apr · 23 September 21 March equinox · 21 Oct 22 Feb · 21 Nov 21 Jan · 22 December solstice

this is just a simple coincidence and question whether our forefathers had the right instruments or knowledge to be able to align a temple like Mnajdra with such precision. Another point brought up by those who oppose the solar-alignment theory is that out of so many temples on the Maltese islands, only one has such an alignment. If the builders were so concerned they would have built more than one temple with similar alignments.

It is an enigma that continues. After numerous sunrises at Mnajdra in the last three years, observing and photographing the 'sundial' at work, it would seem that our society underestimates the intelligence of our forefathers. Mankind of 5,300 years ago reasoned, lived and worshipped in an entirely different way than people do today. Archaeology, anthropology and sociology may create a closer understanding of early customs but many mysteries still remain. The one answer which becomes clear is that humanity may not be as 'advanced' as people think.

The sun is as powerful a force today as it has been for many millennia. Long may it continue to shine.

EXACTLY AS THE SUN APPEARS OVER THE HILL OPPOSITE THE TEMPLE
OF MNAJDRA 1, A RAY OF SUNLIGHT ENTERS THE PORTAL AND LIGHTS
UP THE MAIN AXIS OF THE BUILDING. THIS HAPPENS ONLY TWICE A
YEAR, ON 21 MARCH AND 23 SEPTEMBER, THE EQUINOX DAYS.

Restaurants and bars in the Maltese Islands often serve a delicious locally made peppered cheeselet. Many might not know that they are tasting what is considered to be the most popular cheese – *ġbejniet*, pronounced jb-ay-ni-ert. The cheese is prepared as it was centuries ago.

In rural households it is made and served in a variety of ways and restaurants offer the cheese with salads and in specially prepared dishes. The best and the larger qualities are produced in Gozo, although many Maltese farmers also produce *ġbejniet*. In the past the cheeselets were made with goat, sheep or cow milk, according to what the household could afford. Today only best quality sheep's milk is used.

Locals still milk their sheep according to tradition. The sheep have lambs twice a year, in autumn (so called Christmas lambs) and in spring (Easter lambs). The best milk is obtained from sheep that have Easter lambs, because at this time of year pastures are greener. Another local tradition associated with the production of the best quality milk is to have the sheep milked in the months that have an 'r' in their name. That is in *Jannar, Frar, Marzu, April* (January, February, March, April) and in *Settembru, Ottubru, Novembru, Diċembru* (September, October, November and December). The months that do not have an 'r'– *Mejju, Ġunju, Lulju, Awwissu* (May, June, July and August) – will not yield good quality milk needed to make the cheese.

The actual making of the *ġbejniet* is pretty simple. The main ingredient, besides, of course, milk, is a substance called *qtar*, literally meaning drops. These drops are made from whey, locally known as *xorrox*. This liquid oozes out of the cheeselets as they slowly solidify. The *xorrox* is collected from the dish in which the cheese has been placed to solidify, and is placed in a high bowl.

A salted stomach of a new-born lamb is immersed and left in the *xorrox* for about three days. This causes the *xorrox* to thicken and become the *qtar*. The stomach is washed in running water and placed in salt. The *qtar* is kept in a cool place in an air-tight bottle.

The milking of the sheep takes place immediately before the cheese is prepared. The warm milk is placed in a bowl – preferably made of terracotta – and whilst stirring, the *qtar* is slowly poured in. The amount of *qtar* varies according to the consistency of the milk. It must be precisely measured or the milk will coagulate too much.

The milk becomes curdled and the curd, *baqta*, is left to settle in the bowl for a few minutes before being poured into cup-like moulds with mesh sides. Today the moulds are made of (hygienic) plastic, whereas in years gone by they used to be made of cane, and had to be steamed after every use. The moulds are filled to the brim with the curd and each full *qaleb* (singular) is placed in a low dish. As the cheeselets lie in their *qwieleb* (plural) to thicken, they are taken out, turned and put back three times, and a pinch of salt is sprinkled on to each. The evaporated liquid that oozes out of the curd is collected in a low dish ready to make more *qtar*.

Once each cheeselet hardens enough and does not break, the fresh cheese is ready.

Ġbejniet friski (fresh cheeselets)
These are just that. Fresh cheeselets taken out of the *qwieleb*. They are served as soft, and are delicious when spread over freshly baked warm bread, or added to various broths and pies. It is important not to mistake the *ġbejniet friski* for *rikotta* (cottage) cheese. When spread or put in a pie, they look very alike, but the taste is different.

Ġbejniet moxxi (dried cheeselets) are produced by allowing the fresh cheeselets to dry. The cheeselets are placed on a sort of cane frame, that is slid into a box whose sides are covered with a fine mesh. The box is built to hold several stacked frames and is made of wood. It is usually found – sheltered from strong winds and direct sunlight – on a low roof of the house or on a sheep pen. When the cheese was prepared in nearly every household and the amounts produced were smaller, housewives dried the cheese on a window sill, instead of a cheese box. People today wonder when they see two supports, seemingly supporting nothing, under windows in old houses. These used to hold a thin slab of stone or wooden plank on which the cheese was placed to dry under a fine net.

The time needed for drying is a matter of taste. Some leave the centre of the cheeselet soft, with the outside slightly hard, or leave it longer to harden completely. Normally the cheese should not become too hard, but in some villages it is left to harden completely and used for grating on food, especially pasta dishes.

Ġbejniet moxxi are served in sandwiches, whole, or even melted instead of mozzarella on pizzas or baked macaroni.

Ġbejniet tal-bżar (peppered cheeselets) are left to dry and then washed in lukewarm water. When dry they are washed well in red wine vinegar and put one at a time into a mixture of freshly ground pepper and some coarse sea salt. The cheeselet is turned several times in the mixture until it becomes completely covered with the fine pepper. It is then placed in a jar, and more vinegar is poured in. The jar is sealed and is shaken well.

Left to soak for some weeks, the cheeselets absorb the taste of the pepper and vinegar. Many inexperienced

people try to produce their own *ġbejniet tal-bżar* (also known as *ġbejniet maħsula*, washed cheeselets) with usually poor results. The real peppered cheese can be recognised by breaking the cheeselet in two and observing the small air bubbles in the core which should shed a 'tear'.

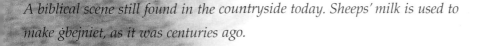

A biblical scene still found in the countryside today. Sheeps' milk is used to make ġbejniet, as it was centuries ago.

Underwater **Malta**

There's more to Malta Gozo and Comino than meets the naked eye. Armed with a mask, the sea around the islands is breathtakingly beautiful. Malta offers a wide variety of sports. And being islands, water sports are, naturally, extremely popular and, above all, safe. No Jaws around here.

As the brochures say, so why not take the plunge and snorkel in the Blue Lagoon, off Comino, or scuba dive to one of the superb dive sites off Gozo. The azure sea around the Maltese archipelago is renowned for its clarity and cleanliness.

The Maltese islands, especially Gozo, offer spectacular scuba diving sites with some of the clearest, unpolluted water in the Mediterranean. An added bonus is that diving in Malta is a year-round sport; during winter the sea temperature rarely drops below 13° Celsius.

Gozo is the diver's paradise, with shallow and deep dives easily accessible from virtually any point on the island. The most attractive features are the numerous underwater caves, some as large as 'sports halls', as well as prolific marine life. Complementing nature's own curiosities are several wrecks, both aircraft and ships that have been designated dive sites.

There are several officially licensed dive centres on the islands, to cater for both the experienced diver and beginner. The centres also rent out equipment and offer qualified instruction for beginners. Most offer four or five day novice courses which covers theoretical work, snorkelling, life-saving and basic scuba diving. Longer sports courses includes more theoretical work plus a series of major dives.

An added attraction for prospective divers is the cost: it is cheaper to learn the sport in Malta or Gozo than virtually any other centre in the Mediterranean.

For experienced divers there are also half-day or full-day accompanied boat dives, night dives, and should they prefer to explore alone without the guidance of a leader, they can hire the full gear for a six day period.

A selection of the islands' most popular **DIVE SITES**

MALTA

Ahrax Point

This is on the north-eastern point of Malta. The entry point is a narrow inlet with depths from three to 10 metres. A 10 minute snorkel gets to the point where two options present themselves – to the left, a reef rich in marine life and an impressive drop-off and, to the right, an underwater entrance into a large cave.

Anchor Bay

This is an ideal location when strong north-easterly winds prevent diving in many other areas. Entry to the water is from a pier. The bottom slopes gradually, reaching depths of 28 metres. There is a large cave to explore and the bottom is rich in red algae.

Ċirkewwa

Situated in the north of the island, this location has long been a favourite among local divers, mainly for its impressive drop-off from eight to 30 metres. The area boasts a picturesque arch and a number of caves.

Għar Lapsi

A fishing hamlet located on the southern coast of Malta. Access to the water is easy. Within a few strokes from the entry point is a shallow system of underwater caves lit up with beams of sunlight from the numerous exits. The Għar Lapsi area is mostly in the 15 to 20 metre depth and offers a large area of parallel reefs and depressions with most of the typical marine fauna of the Mediterranean.

Merkanti Reef

This reef lies off St Julian's Bay. A boat dive is recommended although stronger swimmers can easily reach it from land. The many nooks and crannies house a variety of fish life and other good photographic opportunities.

Qawra Point

This is the southern tip of St Paul's Bay. A large Roman anchor was recovered from the sea in this area. The profile drops slowly at first and the monotony of posidonia meadows gives way to a steep slope to 40 metres. Here many weird-shaped sponges show their magnificence by the light of a torch. A large C-shaped cave often inhabited by brown meagre and bream completes this long dive.

Wied iż-Żurrieq

The steep slope of the valley continues underwater. The bottom is strewn with rocks which must have been carried there over the centuries. At the right of the mouth of the valley there is a small cave. The bottom falls to 30 metres plus. The location comes to its full glory at night as the multitude of crabs hidden during the day venture forth.

GOZO

Reqqa Point

This is the northernmost tip of Gozo. The beach road is rough, the entry is tricky with a strong swell, but it is a fantastic dive. The reef consists of a parapet at a depth of 30 metres and then a drop to 60 metres. However, there is an excellent vantage point at 15 metres. Here one is literally in a cloud of small fish feeding on the nutrient-rich waters. Large shoals of dentex have feeding frenzies, groupers are large and plentiful. Added to this, there are large caves and the water is deep.

Dwejra Point

Dwejra is one of the most spectacular dive sites in Malta, with deep water (60 metres) and many caves and arches. The most dramatic is the 35 metre long tunnel that opens from the Inland Sea to the open sea, where the bottom drops suddenly. The clear waters and depths can be deceptive.

Mġarr ix-Xini

Mġarr ix-Xini is a narrow inlet with tall cliffs either side reaching down to a depth of 30 metres. It is a very popular dive site with photographers due to a variety of species of fish, from gurnard, stargazers and even seahorses. There is also a cave, inside which one can surface.

COMINO

Irqieqa Point

A thin strip of land on the south-western tip of Comino with a sheer drop-off to 40 metres. The water is clear and the cold currents from the depths support large shoals of sardines and bogue that are preyed upon by amberjacks, dentex and, sometimes, tuna. The boulder strewn depths reveal families of bream and brown meagre.

St Marija caves

These are an ideal second dive location for those who have made the boat trip to Comino and want an interesting shallow location. The caves are very pretty and for the underwater photographer the possibilities are endless. Octopus, moray eels, small groupers and countless small fish make this a delightful dive.

The Grand Master's Palace in Valletta – the seat of his power, and the place where he lived, worked, and played under a single large roof – was completed soon after the city was built in the late 16th century.

Palace of the **Grand Masters**

The Grand Master at the time Valletta was being established was Jean l'Eveque de la Cassiere, and tradition has it that the site was given to his Order by the noble Maltese family of Sceberras, on perpetual leasehold. The annual payment was to be five grains of wheat and a glass of water from the well in the courtyard.

The offer was to be made by the Grand Master himself, in the hall of the Gran Consiglio, which is now the hall of St Michael and St George.

The Tapestry Council Chamber – the most beautiful room in Malta. The Gobelins, from designs in the Cabinet du Roi Louis XIV were presented by Grand Master Ramón Perellos y Roccaful (1697–1720). The Lascaris period frieze above and the soffit are both noteworthy.

The building was designed by the noted Maltese architect, Gerolamo Cassar. The stone corbels which support the balconies carry the escrutcheons of the Order of St John, and of the various Grand Masters. In the great central courtyard stands a bronze statue purported to be of Neptune, which was brought there from its original home at the fishmarket during the British governorship of Sir Gaspard Le Marchant. Recent research has, however, shown that the iconography of the head is of Andrea Doria, the Italian admiral famed for his successes at sea and much given to posing as Neptune. The figleaf which shields his privacy, and the trident, are thought to have been later additions. Three expansive corridors on the main floor carry magnificent ceilings of painted canvas. The one in the entrance corridor was executed in 1724 by the Italian master Nicolo Nasoni da Siena, in the time of Grand Master Manoel de Vilhena.

The Hall of St Michael and St George was used by the Grand Masters on solemn occasions and for state functions. The walls of this hall were then covered in red damask and hung with large mirrors to enhance the effect. A frieze of frescoes, which is still in place, depicts scenes from the Great Siege of Malta in 1565. It is the early 17th century work of Matteo Perez d'Aleccio. In a tableau designed to strike awe into even the most fearless of hearts, the Grand Master would sit enthroned beneath a large crucifix at the far end of the hall, wearing his black robe with a large white cross on the front, and a biretta. Above him was a canopy of crimson velvet, with a heavy gold fringe. On either side of him sat the Prior of the Conventual Church, and the Bishop of Malta. The Vice-Chancellor of the Order sat with two assistant priests at an ebony table close by. Officials stood at hand, and ranged around the hall, seated in large gilt armchairs, sat the Conventual bailiffs of the Order, ranked according to seniority, with their lieutenants and Grand Crosses, all wearing their black mantles with a white cross emblazoned across the front.

The panels on the ministrels' gallery show perhaps a logical choice for a celibate order of Knights – the creation of Adam, his suffusion with life, the creation of Eve, the fall from grace, and the expulsion from Eden. Included with these, inexplicably, is the building of the Ark. The panels are said to have been brought from Rhodes by the Knights, after their expulsion and flight to Malta. They were originally in the private chapel of the Grand Master, but were later removed to the great hall. The dining-room and the state drawing-room were paved, as were most of the public rooms, with marble in the 19th century when the palace served as the British Governor's offices. Today they are the offices of the President of the Republic.

In the state drawing-room, there is a frieze of frescoes showing eight scenes

The elegant Neptune Fountain was erected at the Marina in 1615 by Grandmaster Alof de Wignacourt to commemorate the completion of the aqueduct – an ambitious project aimed at bringing water to Valletta. The bronze statue of Neptune, or 'the giant' as it was more popularly known, holds a triton in his right hand, the traditional symbol of his lordship over the seas and the Grand Master's escutcheon shield in his left hand. The fountain was extremely popular with port workers and seamen, it also attracted a number of artists, Louis du Cros, Guintotardi... who sought to portray the lively scenes around it. In 1858 during the governorship of Sir John Gaspard Le Marchant, the statue was moved to the lower courtyard of the Magisterial Palace where it still stands today.

Below: *The President of Malta's private study is in constant and almost daily use. It is not open to the public, and is kept up in Grand Magisterial style with good 18th century furniture and fine pictures from the 17th and 18th centuries.*

Opposite page: *Rooms off this corridor lead to the Palace Chapel and the Grand Masters' summer apartment. Light slashes in to brighten up the full-length portrait of Grand Master Manuel de Rohan Polduc by the French court painter Antoine Favray (1706–1798).*

from the history of the Order of St John, and twelve sombre seated figures from the Old Testament. Some of the most beautiful paintings in the palace are in this room. They include full-length portraits of the Empress Catherine of Russia, Grandmaster Philippe Villiers de l'Isle Adam, Grandmaster Alof de Wignacourt, Louis XVI and Louis XIV of France. A frieze of frescoes in the anteroom – the so-called Yellow Room – depicts eight important events from the early history of the Order. Symbolic figures represent War, Fury, Kindness, Magnanimous Daring and Honour. In what was once the Grand Master's bedroom, there is a low alcove where the bed stood. A frieze of paintings on canvas shows scenes from the Old Testament. The ceiling carries an oil painting of the Blessed Virgin. In the former private chapel of the Grand Master, there is a floor of majolica tiles, and a ceiling of white and gold with gilt rosettes, which carries the arms of

Grand Master de Verdale. There is a frieze of gold fleur-de-lys, and another frieze of 15th century guache paintings showing scenes from the life of St John the Baptist.

One of the most impressive sights today is the Council Chamber hung with priceless Gobelin tapestries. These were made to the order of Grand Master Perellos in the late 17th century and are among the most celebrated Gobelin

tapestries in existence. They show animals and exotic plants, and are based on paintings given to Louis XIV of France by a Prince of Nassau. The arms of Perellos are worked into the border. Apart from the tapestries, there are several works of art to be seen. These include a frieze of oil paintings of the naval battles fought by the Knights, with symbolic figures representing Religion, Charity, Virtue,

Above: *A view of Prince Albert's Courtyard. The door leads out into Old Theatre Street under the arcade of the library of the Magisterial Order.*

Opposite: *Grand Master Pinto's clock tower with its variety of moving parts and dials, it was the finest clock on the Island in the 18th century.*

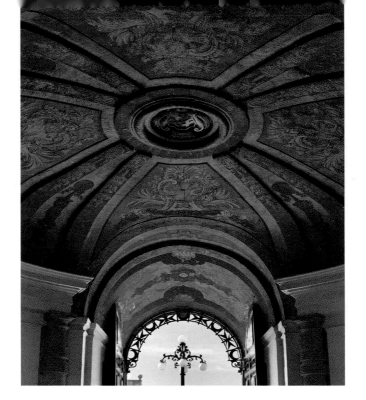

Manhood, Vocation, Providence, Magnanimity, Naval Victory, Hope, and Justice. This chamber was the setting for sittings of the Council of the Order, then of the Council of Government, and later of the Maltese parliament. Parliament today sits elsewhere in the building, in a more spacious hall.

The Armoury in the lower area of the palace owes its origin to a statute of Grand Master de la Sengle, in 1555. He declared all arms of fallen Knights to be the property of the Common Treasury. In the time of Grand Master Pinto, in the 18th century, the Armoury had enough arms for 25,000 men, or so it is said. But the procurators of the Common Treasury in 1763 declared that the Commandant of the Artillery was to clear out all old and obsolete arms, and that the Armoury was to be used only for new arms and armour, which had recently arrived from France. By the end of that century, after Napoleon had forced the Knights out of Malta and, in turn, the French were forced to depart with the arrival of the British, the arms and armour lay forgotten, many of the best items having been plundered.

In 1900, the Governor, Lord Grenfell, sent for Sir Guy Francis Laking, the Keeper of the King's Armoury, who catalogued a full 5,721 pieces. But the havoc of World War II was to wreak its damage, and undo the good done. The arms and armour were stored underground, and suffered terribly from the years of damp conditions. When they were taken out, it took five years of work to have them cleaned and arranged.

The items now on display include a full-length panoply made for Grand

Master Martin Garzes at the end of the 16th century. It is considered to be the work of Sigismund Wolf of Landshut, who was armourer to Philip II of Spain. Another noteworthy item is the full suit of armour worn by Grand Master Alof de Wignacourt, which is made in the Italian fashion (1610–1620). Its decor is rich and lavish, with gold damascening and engraving. This is considered to be one of the finest 17th century suits of armour in existence.

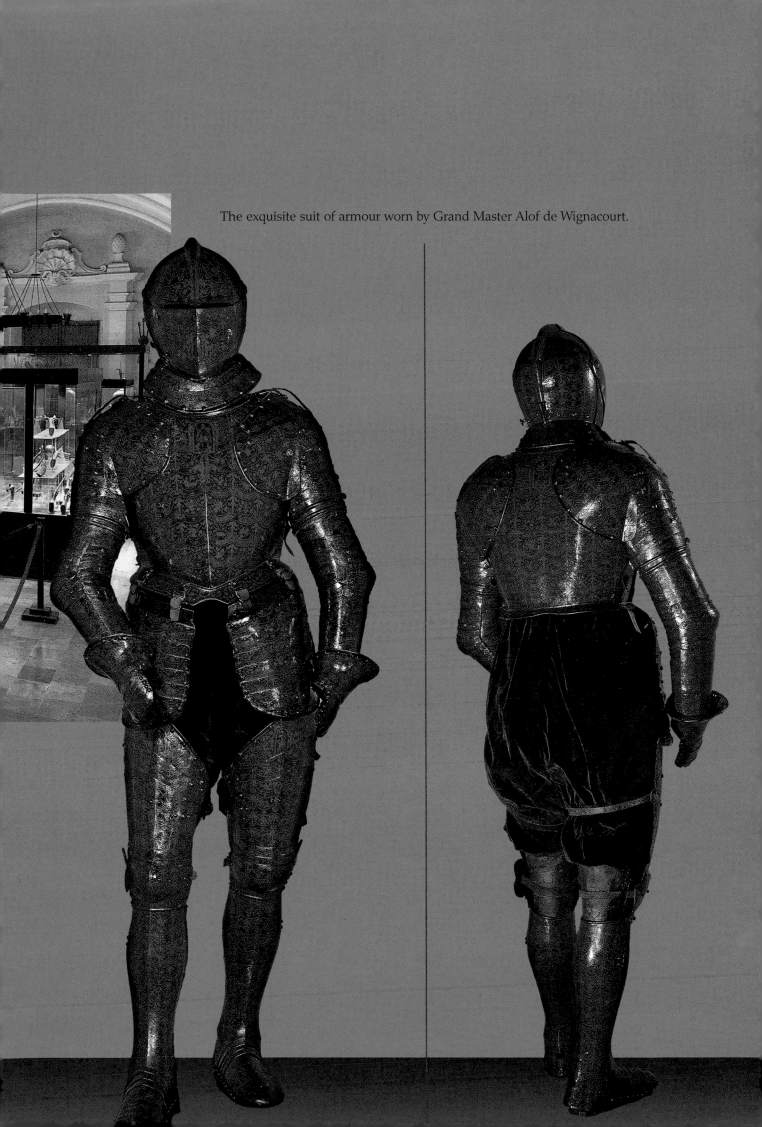

The exquisite suit of armour worn by Grand Master Alof de Wignacourt.

A Gem of a **House**

The Inquisitor's Palace at Girgenti, now the Summer residence of the Prime Ministers of Malta, is perhaps the epitome of elegant simplicity. Delightfully situated in the heart of Malta's countryside, it is truly a haven from modern day life.

CLOSE TO SIĠĠIEWI, AT THE SOUTHERN END OF THE ISLAND, IS THE FERTILE LITTLE VALLEY OF GIRGENTI. AT ITS HEAD IS A FLAT, ROCKY LEDGE, FROM WHICH THE GROUND FALLS SHARPLY BELOW IN WHAT IS A PRECIPICE IN MINIATURE.

On the ledge, which in summer is cool but which in the winter is buffetted by every wind that blows, stands the gem of a house – plain, harmonious, restrained.

Girgenti was built by Inquisitor Onorato Visconti in 1625 and commands a superb view of the surrounding countryside. Its gardens are watered by a number of springs, the main one being that of Għajn il-Kbir, which also irrigates the valley of Girgenti below. Its chapel, dedicated to San Carlo Borromeo, was built by Inquisitor (later Cardinal) Angelo Durini in 1763.

The façade consists of three blocks which lie in one continuous face with recessed panels and plain projecting strips marking the vertical and horizontal divisions. The window surrounds consist of similar plain strips whilst the central axis is accented by a balustrated balcony over the door and a high semicircular-headed French window in the first floor. Good proportions, a clear articulation and an interesting broken skyline produce a pleasing effect so that, although plain, the façade is neither monotonous nor perceptibly severe.

It is worth noting the effectiveness of the single top windows in the two wings. The ground floor plan originally consisted of seven rooms built in a row overlooking the beautiful valley. Three of these rooms, to the right of the entrance hall, now form what is called the Long Room, the principal reception room. At the back of this is a narrow passage which is connected by a graceful loggia to the charming little chapel, which is now the Dining Room.

To the left of the entrance hall is a small study and a serving room which leads to the old kitchen.

The first floor extends over the whole of the ground floor. It includes the Library which is a beautiful high ceilinged room with windows in three of its four walls. This floor also contains the main bedroom with its private terrace, as well as a secondary bedroom and Reading Room.

The second floor only extends over the right wing and contains two bedrooms. What appears to be a second floor over the left wing has been taken up by the Library's high ceiling.

From 1625 to 1798, when the French regime suppressed the Inquisition, Girgenti was the summer residence of Malta's Inquisitors. The Maltese Inquisition had as one of its principal tasks keeping the peace between the other two religious powers on these islands: the Bishop and the Grand Master. Of the 41 Inquisitors who used this house, 26 later became Cardinals and two became Popes, reigning as Alexander VII and Innocent XII respectively.

During the British period Girgenti served initially as the summer residence of the Lieutenant Governors of Malta. In the Second World War it was used as one of the stores for the National Museum's collection. It fell into total disrepair in the 1970s and was fully restored between 1988 and 1990, when it became the official country residence of the Prime Ministers of Malta.

Maritime showcase

Some 10 metres from the waters of
Dockyard Creek with its yacht marina
in the Grand Harbour, and only a few
metres from Fort St Angelo, stands the
former Royal Naval Bakery. This superb
building is on the site of the Order's
arsenal, three covered slipways – the
Galley Arches – where the superb war
galleys of the Order of St John were
maintained and victualled.
With a keen eye for history William
Scamp, an architect and engineer of
enormous talent employed by the
Royal Navy, was called upon to design
a bakery that would supply the entire
Mediterranean Fleet with its daily
requirements of biscuits and bread.
Soon after drydock No 1 was
completed in 1841, the Galley Arches
were levelled and the foundations of

the bakery laid down. Work was completed by 1845 and the bakery became operational. (In the meantime, Scamp had been called in to help with the engineering of the new St Paul's Anglican Cathedral in Valletta, that was in danger of collapsing. His young daughter became the first person to be baptised in the new church). After decades of service, when the British garrison departed, the historic building was decommissioned – as the National Maritime Museum.

As visitors to the Museum will appreciate, in its days as a bakery it was the most technologically advanced factory in the Mediterranean, and probably in the whole of the Royal Navy too. Motive power was provided by two large steam engines, though sadly, the equipment was sold off for scrap.

One of the first things that strike the visitor is the sheer size of the building. The ground floor houses the marine engineering section – and the heavyweight interest here is the eight ton engine from the grab dredger *Anadrian*, a vessel built purposely for Malta in 1951 by Fergusson Brothers of Port Glasgow in Scotland. The engine is installed and working around it, but not as cramped as in the actual engine room are the various ancillaries, and, of course, a mass of other interesting and noteworthy pieces of engineering. On a floor above, nobly supported by the first cast iron pillars to be imported to Malta is the mock-up of the *Anadrian* bridge. The rest of this hall is dedicated to traditional Maltese sea crafts and other objects that indicate Malta's long-standing maritime vocation. Organised into thematic and chronological sectors, the Main Hall exhibits from archeological times to the end of the knights' period. The entrance to the main hall is surrounded by Roman period amphorae and a fine collection of Roman anchor 'stocks' made of lead, found locally. One has been rebuilt and gives a good idea as to how large Roman vessels were. Nearby are a couple of corroded iron anchors found on the seabed from galleys of the Order. The museum has around sixty model boats and ships, most of which are on show. One, 3 metres long, is a fully rigged third rate ship-of-the-line belonging to the Order in the 18th century, and close by is the ceremonial barge of the Grand Master Adrien de Wignacourt, built late in the 17th century. There are some notable paintings, the most spectacular being *Our Lady of the Fleet* by Antonello Riccio, reputed to be an ex voto of the famous battle of Lepanto in 1571. The picture was executed in 1575, the oldest painting in the museum.

There is also a good section of naval gunnery, with a fine assortment of weapons and range finding equipment. The collection from the Vice-Admiralty Court – set up in 1815 by Governor Maitland in the Palace in Valletta – for trial by jury, for the first time in Malta, pirates and similar villains is well displayed, with seals, manuscripts and a fine silver oar-mace. These trials were discontinued in 1860. The trial for piracy of Captain Delano is well documented. The customs and excise section holds an interesting collection of weights and measures in excellent condition, some are made of brass and some of wood; there are measuring rods, seals, a couple of uniforms and the old bell from the Customs House, dated 1873. One of the star exhibits is the figurehead from the famous first rate British ship-of-the-line, the *Hibernia*. She was launched on 17 November 1804, spent much of her active life as flagship of the Mediterranean Fleet, and was base flagship from 1855 until 1902, when she was then broken up in Malta. The figurehead has great sentimental value for the Maltese and was displayed locally until being taken back to the Royal Naval Museum at Portsmouth in 1971.

In July 1994 it was returned to Malta for permanent exhibition at the Maritime Museum.

How trotting became popular in Malta

A day at the RACES

Horse racing has always been a popular sport for the Maltese. Until the middle of the last century, horse riding and racing were confined to public roads, while races were organised by a number of parishes, as part of their village feast.

In 1868 a small number of gentlemen, mostly military and naval officers together with other members of the Malta Union Club, decided to build a racecourse.

A working body, called the Malta Racing Committee, was set up and the Marsa area was chosen as the site of the proposed race track.

Funds to realise this dream were raised and within 12 months the first race meeting was held over two days, the 12 and 13 April 1869. The card consisted of six events open to thoroughbreds, and the Malta Grand National Steeplechase – a two mile race open to English, Arab, Barbs and Spanish horses. As the trotting horse was still in trials stages in Europe and the rest of the world, trotting races were not yet introduced.

The newly formed club was then known as the Malta Race Club and the official controlling body as the Malta Race Committee. Club records of those early days are scant, but what is known is that all jockeys were amateurs and meetings were officiated on a *gratis et amoris* basis.

By the end of the 19th century the big muscled French trotter had matured into its present form, while in the United States the American standard-bred was already racing at high speeds although over shorter distances than its European counterpart. The appeal of the trotting horse in Europe and America was being felt all over the racing world.

Trotting tracks were being built everywhere and the popularity of this 'new' sport rose throughout Europe, except in Great Britain where, apart from having the best flat racetracks in the world, the people tended to be more conservative.

By 1910 the sport had become so popular in France that the number of trotting tracks outnumbered the traditional race courses, and trotting

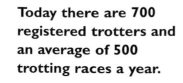

Today there are 700 registered trotters and an average of 500 trotting races a year.

became the number one equine racing sport in that country.

This phenomenal popularity was also being felt in other countries such as Sweden, Norway, Finland, Denmark, Italy and Germany.

In most states in the USA, trotting was considered more popular than the conventional flat gallop, while in Australasia trotting was the number one equine sport.

All this may come as a surprise to many as in the past we all were led to believe that trotting was the less popular form of horse racing, probably through reading British texts which referred to the flats and thoroughbred racing.

But how did trotting become so popular in Malta after a long history of British rule?

For the first 60 years of horse racing in Malta no history of official trotting races were recorded. Probably the first trotters to arrive in Malta were in the 1930–34 period when the popular Arab and Barb ponies were imported from Tunisia.

In the following years some wealthy gentlemen imported the first French trotters.

As most of the Malta Race Committee was British, it took quite some time for it to accept the trotter as a race horse. At first only races between two trotters were held, but soon the growing popularity of these races and the shortage of lightweight jockeys prompted the club to introduce one trotting race at each race meeting. With the outbreak of the Second World

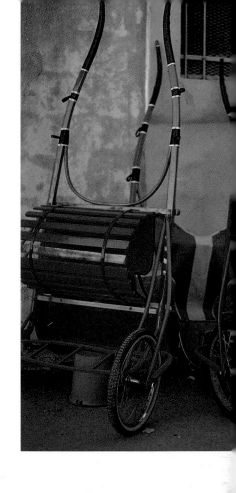

War racing stopped completely. Racing resumed on 29 December 1945 with a few horses on the card. A year later several horses were imported from Tunisia and France, and trotting restarted.

The old racecourse, meanwhile, measured one and three quarter miles (2,668 meters) and was the longest in Europe, but it was not suitable for trotting; consequently the sport was given backseat status.

By 1965 trotting was once again gaining popularity, mainly due to the shortage of good thoroughbreds and the lack of lightweight jockeys. However, a lot of good trotters were being imported from France and Italy and by 1967 the number of trotting races outnumbered flat races. By 1973 only two flat races were held from a total of eight on the card.

In 1974 the Committee of Stewards, by now made up mainly of Maltese, decided to rebuild the racecourse and shorten it to international trotting standards, very similar to the Agnano track in Naples, Italy.

In March 1981 the new track was inaugurated, opening a new era for the trotter. The thoroughbred was reduced to an all time low in the popularity stakes.

Today there are only a few thoroughbreds in Malta, and only a few flat races are held annually.

Today, there are an average of 500 trotting races a year, with 700 trotters currently registered with the Malta Racing Club.

Races are generally held on Sundays,

alternate Saturdays and most public holidays, with attendances averaging 4,000 spectators. Trotting has now become the number one spectator sport in Malta.

In 1991, Malta was accepted as a full member of the Union Europeénne du Trot (UET) and trotting races are held under international rules.

In recent years Malta has witnessed a steady increase in the number of horses imported from Scandinavia, particularly from Sweden.

This fresh bloodstock by no small means is contributing to racing in Malta, as a lot of classy horses are recording fast times, thus prompting local owners and trainers to import still better horses. The upshot, of course, is that standards are constantly being raised and a visit to the Marsa track a must for visitors.

The bush that clings tenaciously to the face of bastion walls, and
is the bane of the conservator's working life, yields a delicacy which is
sold in the food halls of major department stores, supermarkets and
delicatessens all over Europe. It is the caper *(Capparis spinosa)*, known to
the Maltese as *kappar*. Growing wild all over the southern Mediterranean,
it takes its name from the Latin, capparis, and is known as kapparis in
Greek and capres in French.

The bush does not favour good terrain or fertile soil, but grows best in
rocky territory, showing a strong preference for rugged surroundings.

Caper bushes flourish on bastion walls and grow wild in rubble walls in the countryside. The caper buds turn into the most beautiful and delicate of flowers.

Capers can be cultivated, grown from seed or from cuttings, but ironically they do best when they are left to look after themselves. Large, full plants sprout in the most unlikely places and thrive on the little water they extract from the natural environment. The buds that escape the hands of the caper-pickers develop into beautiful purple and white flowers nestling in dark green foliage. The flowers are short-lived, and do not take kindly to being placed in a vase.

Capers sold in jars are not the fruit of the plant. They are the unopened flower bud, picked in the summer months by families equipped with plastic bags and unlimited patience. They are scalded and placed in brine in air-tight, sterile jars. They are left there for at least two months. A test for the correct salinity of the brine is to place an uncooked egg still in its shell in the brine. If the egg floats, then the solution is perfect.

The capers are a favourite in southern Mediterranean recipes. They are used in sauces, particularly for fish, and yield a marvellous, inimitable flavour. In Malta they are used in summer salads, in fillings concocted for bread rolls, and as a garnish for rich tomato dishes.

Local supermarkets sell professionally-packed capers imported from Italy, but many still prefer those picked and prepared locally.

Little old ladies who sold capers prepared by members of their own families on street corners, have now become a rare sight. Only a few years ago, the cry of *"Kappar!"* was part of the morning hustle and bustle, and housewives would emerge from their homes to buy a jar, and perhaps a handful of parsley, from the street vendor.

Times change but fortunately, capers do not.

ST PAUL'S BAY TOWER BUILT IN 1609 BY GRAND MASTER ALOF DE WIGNACOURT

*For centuries the Maltese Islands were
exposed to raids by passing corsairs who
would kidnap the locals to sell as slaves
and ransack the countryside.*

THE COASTAL **SENTINELS**

*For centuries the Maltese Islands were
exposed to raids by passing corsairs who
would kidnap the locals to sell as slaves
and ransack the countryside.*

It was not until the beginning of the
17th century that the Order of St John
embarked on a system of improving the
coastal watch as they had done during
their occupation of Rhodes. The first
watchtower was built in Gozo's main
harbour, Mgarr, to oversee the channel
between Gozo and Comino. It was
financed by the Aragonese Grand
Master, Martin Garzes, who made a
provision for it in his will, and it was
built during the time of Grand Master
Alof de Wignacourt, in 1605. 'This
tower was demolished during the
19th century'.

Wignacourt continued the tower-
building project, and another six went
up along the coast: at St Paul's
Bay (1609), at Marsaxlokk (1610), at
Marsascala (1614), on Comino (1618),
at Marsalforn in Gozo (1614), and at
Xagħra (1620). The last two have also
since been demolished.

The towers were all large, solid,
squarish structures. Troops were
stationed in them only at times of the
greatest danger. The soldiers were
expected to repel the enemy as well as
carry out reconnaissance duties. But in
addition to these garrisoned outposts,
the need for ordinary watchtowers was
deemed as great. Wignacourt's
successor, the Frenchman Jean Lascaris
1636–1657, ordered the construction of
another six towers: at St George's Bay,
at Qawra, at Għajn Tuffieħa, at Ġnejna
Bay, at Blat il-Mogħża and at Wied
iż-Żurrieq. These were all built in 1637,
and their architectural style reflects a
marked departure from the massive,
garrisoned style of Wignacourt's time.

TWO NEIGHBOURING TOWERS BUILT ON MALTA'S NORTH-WEST COAST BY JEAN LASCARIS IN 1637

The Lascaris towers were not designed to resist a large enemy force, but simply to survey the horizon and to relay warning signals to the nearest garrison. There was more yet to be done for the country's security. The Aragonese Grand Master, Martino de Redin, who succeeded Lascaris, pointed out the inadequacy of the coastal defences. Raiders were still able to land unnoticed, and carry out their looting relatively unhindered. De Redin proposed a new scheme, which provided for additional watchtowers, and for new conditions of work for the guards who manned the look-out posts. In 1658 he put forward a long and detailed statement of the prevailing situation, and of his newly devised plan to a meeting of the Order's Council. It was unanimously approved.

De Redin planned 13 new watchtowers, which were built at his own personal expenses at key sites round the island of Malta, between the years 1658–1659. The western coast was already inaccessible to raiders because of the steep cliffs, so no towers were needed here. Elsewhere each tower was built within sight of a neighbouring one, so direct communication could be made on a 24-hour basis. Carrier pigeons were used during the day, and fire signals by night. In this way, alarm signals were relayed from one coastal tower to another, all the way to the Knights' stronghold, Valletta.

Each tower was manned by four

people, a bombardier and three assistants, on 24-hour guard duty rota. Each received a monthly salary, which was paid by the Università of the Città Notabile (Mdina). The towers were each equipped with a small cannon, and the guardsmen carried muskets. Five of these towers have since been demolished, and several of the others have been put to practical use. One such well-known example is the tower on the Sliema promenade, which has given its name to Tower Road, and which is now used as a cafe.

The watchtowers of De Redin and Lascaris had a similar plan: square, with outer battened sides, and no openings at ground floor level. The entrances at ground level which can be seen today are the 19th century additions by the British military forces. On the second level were the living-quarters of the guardsmen, and two look-out windows, one facing towards the sea, the other inland. The only means of access to the tower during the time of the Knights was a rear window, above which is a marble plaque which records the Grand Master's generosity, the year of construction, and the tower's numerical position.

The towers were used by the British infantry units and by the Kings Own Malta Regiment, for defence purposes during World War I and II. After that, they became redundant as far as national security was concerned. Today, they are seen as part of a heritage which must be preserved.